JANUARY 2018

Managing Fragility and Promoting Resilience to Advance Peace, Security, and Sustainable Development

AUTHOR
James Michel

A REPORT OF THE
CSIS PROJECT ON PROSPERITY AND DEVELOPMENT

CSIS | CENTER FOR STRATEGIC &
INTERNATIONAL STUDIES

ROWMAN &
LITTLEFIELD
Lanham • Boulder • New York • London

About CSIS

For over 50 years, the Center for Strategic and International Studies (CSIS) has worked to develop solutions to the world's greatest policy challenges. Today, CSIS scholars are providing strategic insights and bipartisan policy solutions to help decisionmakers chart a course toward a better world.

CSIS is a nonprofit organization headquartered in Washington, D.C. The Center's 220 full-time staff and large network of affiliated scholars conduct research and analysis and develop policy initiatives that look into the future and anticipate change.

Founded at the height of the Cold War by David M. Abshire and Admiral Arleigh Burke, CSIS was dedicated to finding ways to sustain American prominence and prosperity as a force for good in the world. Since 1962, CSIS has become one of the world's preeminent international institutions focused on defense and security; regional stability; and transnational challenges ranging from energy and climate to global health and economic integration.

Thomas J. Pritzker was named chairman of the CSIS Board of Trustees in November 2015. Former U.S. deputy secretary of defense John J. Hamre has served as the Center's president and chief executive officer since 2000.

CSIS does not take specific policy positions; accordingly, all views expressed herein should be understood to be solely those of the author(s).

ISBN: 978-1-4422-8047-2 (pb); 978-1-4422-8048-9 (eBook)

Center for Strategic & International Studies
1616 Rhode Island Avenue, NW
Washington, DC 20036
202-887-0200 | www.csis.org

Rowman & Littlefield
4501 Forbes Boulevard
Lanham, MD 20706
301-459-3366 | www.rowman.com

Contents

Acronyms and Abbreviations

ADB	Asian Development Bank
AfDB	African Development Bank
AGE	Advisory Group of Experts on Peace Operations
CICIG	Comisión Internacional contra la Impunidad en Guatemala (International Commission against Impunity in Guatemala)
CPIA	Country Policy and Institutional Assessment
DAC	Development Assistance Committee of the Organization for Economic Cooperation and Development
DFID	Department for International Development, United Kingdom
EU	European Union
FCS	Fragile and conflict-affected situations or states
FEWS	Famine Early Warning System
FFP	Fund for Peace
g7+	Intergovernmental group of states that have experienced conflict and fragility, which provides a collective voice for those seeking ways out of conflict and fragility
GEMAP	Liberia's Governance and Economic Management Assistance Program
GSDRC	Governance and Social Development Research Centre
HIPPO	High-Level Independent Panel on Peace Operations
HLPF	High-Level Political Forum on Sustainable Development
HN	Host nation
IDA	International Development Association, World Bank
IDP	Internally displaced person
IDPS	International Dialogue on Peacebuilding and Statebuilding
IFC	International Finance Corporation
IMF	International Monetary Fund
INCAF	International Network on Conflict and Fragility

LICUS	Low-Income Countries under Stress
MCC	Millennium Challenge Corporation
MIGA	Multilateral Investment Guarantee Agency
NATO	North Atlantic Treaty Organization
NSC	U.S. National Security Council
OECD	Organization for Economic Cooperation and Development
OPIC	Overseas Private Investment Corporation
PBA	Peacebuilding Architecture
PBC	Peacebuilding Commission
PBSO	Peacebuilding Support Office
RCF	Rapid Credit Facility
SDGs	Sustainable Development Goals
UNDP	UN Development Programme
UNGA	UN General Assembly
USAID	U.S. Agency for International Development
WDR	*World Development Report*

Executive Summary

Societies affected by poor governance, limited institutional capability, low social cohesion, and weak legitimacy tend to exhibit erosion of the social contract, diminished societal resilience, and low levels of economic and human development. They frequently experience high levels of violence and little respect for the rule of law. Adverse spillover effects of their fragility extend beyond national borders, increasing risks of armed conflict, forced migration, the spread of contagious diseases, organized crime, and terrorism.

The Sustainable Development Goals (SDGs) promise that "no-one will be left behind." Yet countries experiencing significant fragility, while amounting to about 20 percent of the world's population, are projected to be home to 80 percent of the world's extremely poor by 2035. On the present trajectory, a growing number of people will be left behind, living in fragile situations.

THE FRAGILITY CONTINUUM

Various definitions and lists of "fragile states" (several are summarized below) have called attention to situations and trends of broad concern. These definitions, indices, and analytical models all consider similar dimensions of fragility: economic, political, security, and social. But while differing in specifics, they produce largely similar results.

The *World Bank* defines a "fragile state" as one having either (a) a composite Country Policy and Institutional Assessment (CPIA) rating of 3.2 or less or (b) the presence of a UN and/or regional peacekeeping or peacebuilding mission during the past three years.

For the *Organization for Economic Cooperation and Development (OECD)*, fragility is "the combination of exposure to risk and insufficient coping capacity of the state, system, and/or communities to manage, absorb, or mitigate those risks."

The *Fund for Peace (FFP)* does not have a formal definition, but uses a set of indicators to measure the performance and experience of 178 countries against 12 indicators relating to cohesion, economic, political, and social and cross-cutting issues.

The *U.S. Agency for International Development (USAID)* describes fragility as referring to "the extent to which state-society relations fail to produce outcomes that are considered to be effective and legitimate."

The *UN Development Programme (UNDP)* regards fragile contexts as including "those countries and territories experiencing armed conflict, emerging from armed conflict, or affected by acute political, social, and economic vulnerability and susceptible to chronic forms of organized criminal violence."

The *g7+* group of conflict-affected states defines fragility flexibly as "a period of time during nationhood when sustainable socio-economic development requires greater emphasis on complementary peacebuilding or statebuilding activities such as building inclusive political settlements, security, justice, jobs, good management of resources, and accountable and fair service delivery."

The *Fragility Study Group*, organized in 2016 by the leaders of the Carnegie Endowment for International Peace, Center for American Security, and U.S. Institute of Peace, defines fragility as "the absence or breakdown of a social contract between people and their government. Fragile states suffer from deficits of institutional capacity and political legitimacy that increase the risk of instability and violent conflict and sap the state of its resilience to disruptive shocks."

The diversity among situations identified as "fragile" is striking. The many variables among fragile situations suggest it is better to address fragility on the facts of each individual case rather than to divide countries facing distinctive challenges into categories of "fragile" and "not fragile." Indications of fragility are evident in many countries at different points along a continuum that extends from crisis to resiliency.

Numerous scholars and practitioners have proposed creative ideas that can help to shape practical and coherent strategies for managing fragility based on the facts of each situation. These ideas include the following:

A focus on key factors: Often only a few key factors determine a country's situation and its position on the continuum. A focus on these key factors may be the most effective way to improve the situation.

A focus on context: Many case studies attribute government shortcomings to *either* insufficient political will *or* insufficient capacity, but do not take the next step to assess which of these two causes is most relevant in a particular context. Where asymmetries in the balance of power among key actors inhibit reforms, more capacity-building assistance is not a sufficient answer. It is necessary to address issues of participation, political commitment, incentives, and preferences and beliefs.

A focus on gaps: Beyond addressing the various indicators of fragility, a focus on gaps in capacity, security, and legitimacy—and the potential conflicts among these gaps—can provide a basis for sound policy.

THE INTERNATIONAL RESPONSE TO FRAGILITY

The international response to fragility has been influenced by three major concerns.

One is the growing resource demands of fragile situations. The need for resources to respond to frequent disasters and conflict situations has given rise to concerns that scarce foreign assistance funds were being diverted away from long-term efforts to promote development and thereby address the underlying causes of conflict.

A second concern is the persistent lack of progress toward development goals by some countries. This has given rise to increased emphasis on improving aid effectiveness. Special attention to the issue of fragility was included in the 2005 Paris Declaration on Aid Effectiveness, the 2008 Accra Agenda for Action, and the 2011 Busan Partnership Declaration.

Third, an alarming increase in terrorist acts has made it more strikingly evident than ever before that fragility is more than a development issue. It also needs to be addressed as a strategic risk to security. This realization has given rise to demands for more comprehensive and coherent strategies to address both the security and the development aspects of fragility.

The search for coherence involves numerous efforts by highly diverse local and international entities with differing mandates, capabilities, perspectives, cultures, expertise, staffing practices, and resources. All responsible international actors want to contribute to a stable environment of peace and opportunity. However, different understandings and perspectives have impeded efficient coordination and complicated the planning and implementation of coherent strategies for realizing shared objectives.

The United States, the European Union, the United Nations, and a host of other international actors have undertaken prodigious efforts to develop and implement effective responses to the complex challenges of fragility. The International Dialogue on Peacebuilding and Statebuilding (IDPS) has brought together conflict-affected states, international donors, international organizations, and civil society representatives. Their New Deal for Engagement in Fragile States focuses on locally identified problems and collaboration with local actors through compacts that promote mutual responsibility. The compacts embrace frequent review and adaptation, building trust, and empowering people to achieve sustainable results.

As experience has been gained, policies and strategies have been reviewed, refined, and revised repeatedly. Efforts to improve the international response continue. In 2016, the members of the IDPS pledged to renew their commitments to the New Deal. UNDP has given primary emphasis in its strategic plan to integrated support for democratic governance, conflict prevention, and peacebuilding. The European Union is implementing a strategic approach to the challenge of "structural fragility," including expanded access to assistance and guarantees. The World Bank has made fragility, conflict, and violence a special theme for the International Development Association (IDA) in 2017–2020. The International Monetary Fund (IMF) adopted a new policy in 2017 on building fiscal capacity in fragile states.

Looking ahead, the UN secretary-general has called on the international community "to connect global efforts for peace and security, sustainable development and human rights, not just in words, but in practice." A high-level meeting of the UN General Assembly in April 2018 will concentrate on sustaining peace. Goal 16 of the SDGs (concerning peaceful and inclusive societies) will be reviewed in depth in the High Level Political Forum on Sustainable Development in 2019.

LESSONS LEARNED AND THE PATH FORWARD

There are reasons why a consistent, effective response to the challenges of fragility has continued to elude the international community:

Fragility has multiple and interrelated dimensions, each of which may vary in severity from time to time and from place to place.

An enormous variety of situations can overwhelm a society's capacity to cope, giving rise to fragility concerns. Fragility tends to be persistent, but some countries have made important progress.

International actors measure the multiple dimensions of fragility in different ways. Some approach fragility from a security perspective. Some view it as a development problem. Differing organizational cultures impede collaboration.

International cooperation has become more complex as the number, variety, and roles of international actors have multiplied and international finance has become far more diversified, with a diminished global role for development assistance.

Despite these difficulties, experience has produced a substantial body of shared knowledge that has attracted wide support:

- The several dimensions of fragility are manifested in particular situations somewhere along a continuum that extends from crisis to resilience.

- The preferred approach is to concentrate on the principal impediments in each situation in a manner that respects the essentially endogenous nature of the process of building a stable and resilient society.

- An inclusive approach with broad participation can help to build popular support and momentum, especially in divided societies.

- International actors should favor whole-of-government approaches that focus on key priorities and benefit from coordinated diplomatic, development, and military input, as appropriate to the context.

- There should be priority for prevention and acting before a crisis erupts.

- Transformation from fragility to resilience takes time, and international engagement needs to continue long enough to give success a chance.

This body of shared knowledge suggests that relationships with countries experiencing fragility should look beyond traditional aid instruments to advance shared objectives. They should also include, as appropriate, diplomatic dialogue, educational and cultural exchanges, trade and investment, private-sector business development, civil society oversight of government performance, and engagement with the security sector.

International and local actors should be open to innovative and creative ideas. Special efforts will be needed to convert declarations of intention to prioritize prevention into effective action. This will require a fundamental elevation of public awareness, supported by committed political leadership.

IMPLICATIONS FOR THE UNITED STATES

The ideas presented in this report for improving the international response to fragility provide opportunities for the United States to improve its own effectiveness in managing fragility and promoting transitions to resilience, including through its leadership in the international community.

The Fragility Study Group suggested a framework for the United States that is strategic, systemic, selective, and sustained. Within this highly commendable framework, the following measures should be considered:

- Abandon the binary typology that treats some countries as fragile and others as not fragile. Instead, recognize that fragility is a multidimensional continuum affecting many countries and bring fragility considerations into the mainstream of international relations.

- Strengthen and streamline coordination mechanisms to minimize fragmentation, facilitate efficiency, and maximize coherence of efforts.

- Build expertise in fragility into the human resource base of the concerned government agencies, including longer assignments, language proficiency, and expanded training opportunities, with career-enhancing incentives.

- Increase emphasis on early warning and early response that can help to prevent deterioration of fragile situations into crisis or conflict.

- Provide leadership through actions to strengthen the international response to fragility, including through implementing the New Deal, encouraging multilateral development institutions to exercise greater flexibility, and improving integration with other international efforts.

OVERALL CONCLUSIONS

This report places the challenges to security and development posed by fragility in the context of centuries-long trends toward declining violence and increased prosperity and freedom. It shows how today's fragile situations represent exceptions to these historic global trends—and potential threats to their continuation.

It also recounts how governments, public and private international organizations, multilateral development banks, private business organizations, and civil society groups have endeavored to improve their policies and strategies and to strengthen coordination among actors who bring differing perspectives to the effort to manage fragility and promote resilience.

Building on past efforts and experience, the report suggests ways in which coordinated international efforts can help to mitigate and prevent fragility. Each fragile situation that is ameliorated will reduce risks, avoid the need for more costly and less promising reactive efforts after a crisis occurs, and, perhaps, demonstrate a pattern of results-oriented collaborative behavior that can be extended to other areas of common endeavor.

Introduction

Poor governance, limited institutional capability, low social cohesion, and weak legitimacy impede and erode the social contract between a state and its citizens and diminish the resilience needed for a society to overcome shocks and chronic weaknesses.[1] These conditions are hostile to sustainable development and pose threats to peace and security.

Countries affected by these phenomena tend to exhibit low levels of economic and human development along with high concentrations of political and economic power. They frequently experience high levels of violence and little respect for human rights and the rule of law. Large segments of the people living in these fragile situations must contend with prolonged insecurity, poverty, and deprivation. They have limited expectations for political voice, economic progress, or social mobility.[2]

In addition, adverse spillover effects of fragility extending beyond national borders can increase risks of armed conflict, forced migration, the spread of contagious disease, organized crime, and terrorism. The threats are widely recognized. For example, the 2015 U.S. National Security Strategy identified "security consequences associated with weak or failing states" as one of the "top

---

1. Resilience is widely recognized as an essential condition for peaceful and productive societies. It has been defined as "the ability of people, households, communities, countries, and systems to mitigate, adapt to, and recover from shocks and stresses in a manner that reduces chronic vulnerability and facilitates inclusive growth." USAID, *Building Resilience to Recurrent Crisis* (Washington, DC: USAID, 2012a), 5, https://www.usaid.gov/sites/default/files/documents /1870/USAIDResiliencePolicyGuidanceDocument.pdf. See also Louise Bosetti, Alexandra Ivanovic, and Menaal Munshey, *Fragility, Risk, and Resilience: A Review of Existing Frameworks* (Tokyo: United Nations University, 2016).

2. Measurements of the incidence of poverty, vulnerability to violence, environmental stress, and limits on government capacities illustrate the strong correlation among these factors. Countries that perform poorly on any one of them tend to perform poorly on all of them. See Timothy Besley and Torsten Persson, "The Pillars of Prosperity Index," in *Pillars of Prosperity: The Political Economics of Development Clusters* (Princeton, NJ: Princeton University Press, 2011a), 310–325; Stephen C. Smith, "The Two Fragilities: Vulnerability to Conflict, Environmental Stress, and Their Interaction as Challenges to Ending Poverty," in *The Last Mile in Ending Extreme Poverty*, ed. Laurence Chandy, Hiroshi Kato, and Homi Kharas (Washington, DC: Brookings Institution Press, 2015), 328–368.

strategic risks to our interests."[3] These risks vary greatly in their nature, severity, geographic scope, and unpredictability, thereby defying formulaic analysis and precluding standardized responses.

International attention has reflected the desire to relieve human suffering and support the aspirations of disadvantaged people for security, well-being, and dignity. This humanitarian response is combined with self-interested concerns about the adverse spillover risks of fragile situations. The combination of motivations about a wide variety of circumstances has produced a continuing debate about many issues: the root causes and drivers of change; the balance among policy interests; the choice of instruments for responding; and appropriate roles of local and international actors. The uncertainties underlying this debate have impeded the formulation and implementation of coherent approaches and effective strategies.

For the most part, attention has been focused on individual countries, although broader geographic contexts are also of concern.[4] The countries of focus have been described by many names over time: difficult partners, low-income countries under stress, countries that are failed and failing, fragile and conflict-affected, poorly performing, precarious, and vulnerable. The issues of fragility have generated an enormous volume of scholarly research, multilateral guidance, policy declarations of governments and organizations, case studies, and evaluations. The very use of the fragility concept and terminology has given rise to political controversy.[5]

This report uses the term "fragility" to refer generally to the combination of poor governance, limited institutional capability, low social cohesion, and weak legitimacy that erodes the social contract and diminishes societal resilience. (In some cases, these conditions impede even the

---

3. White House, *National Security Strategy* (Washington, DC: National Archives, 2015), 2, https://obamawhitehouse .archives.gov/sites/default/files/docs/2015_national_security_strategy_2.pdf. A recent worldwide threat assessment suggests that "poor governance, weak national political institutions, economic inequality, and the rise of violent nonstate actors" will continue to be seen as a strategic risk. See Director of National Intelligence, Worldwide Threat Assessment of the U.S. Intelligence Community, Statement for the Record, Senate Select Committee on Intelligence (May 11, 2017), https://www.dni.gov/files/documents/Newsroom/Testimonies/SSCI%20Unclassified%20SFR%20-%20 Final.pdf. The new National Security Strategy issued in December 2017 addresses fragility in the context of support for aspiring partners "where state weaknesses or failure would magnify threats to the American homeland." White House, *National Security Strategy* (Washington, DC: White House, 2017), 37–40, https://whitehouse.gov/wp-content/uploads /2017/12/NSS-Final-12-18-2017-0905.pdf.

4. Particular attention has been given to Africa and the Middle East. See Enrique Gelbard, *Building Resilience in Sub-Saharan Africa's Fragile States* (Washington, DC: IMF, 2015), http://www.imf.org/en/Publications/Departmental -Papers-Policy-Papers/Issues/2016/12/31/Building-Resilience-in-Sub-Saharan-Africa-s-Fragile-States-42950; Perry Cammack, Michele Dunne, Amr Hamzawy, Marc Lynch, Marwan Muasher, Yezid Sayigh, and Maha Yahya, *Arab Fractures: Citizens, States, and Social Contracts* (Washington, DC: Carnegie Endowment for International Peace, 2017), http://carnegieendowment.org/files/Arab_World_Horizons_Final.pdf.

5. For an indication of the volume of literature on fragility, see the extensive bibliographies in OECD, *States of Fragility 2016* (Paris: OECD, 2016b), http://www.oecd-ilibrary.org/docserver/download/4316101e.pdf?expires=1503687162&id =id&accname=guest&checksum=F238BADDB1ED3A081A57A0BC3DFEADD3; Rachel M. Gisselquist, *Aid, Governance, and Fragility* (Helsinki: UN University World Institute for Development Economics Research, 2014), https://www.wider .unu.edu/sites/default/files/PP2014-Aid%2C%20Governance%20and%20Fragility.pdf. For skeptical views about the motives of policymakers who developed and use the concept of state fragility, see Sonja Grimm, Nicolas Lemay-Hebert, and Olivier Nay, eds., *The Political Invention of Fragile States: The Power of Ideas* (New York: Routledge, 2015).

formation of a social contract or societal resilience.) The following chapters explore the nature of these obstacles to sustainable development, peace, and security; how the international community has defined, measured, and responded to the phenomenon of fragility; how the international response might be made more effective; and implications for the United States.

Chapter 1 describes the historic relationships among fragility, violence, and development. It reviews historical trends toward less violence (despite some recent reversals) and increased human development. In addition, it shows how fragile environments have become the principal exceptions to these positive trends and why they require priority attention by the international community.

Chapter 2 examines the various dimensions of fragility, efforts to define the concept, and approaches for trying to measure fragility in particular situations. It describes the indicators and methodologies used by various organizations that track fragility. Some examples of creative thinking that warrant particular attention in shaping future efforts to prevent deterioration and support recovery are presented as well.

Chapter 3 reviews international responses and perspectives. It examines concerns about resource constraints, aid effectiveness, and the spread of terrorism and criminal violence that have driven international attention to fragility. This chapter describes how various national and international systems have developed responses to the interrelated security and development aspects of this phenomenon, how those responses have differed, and how they have evolved. It reveals a pattern of recurring review and revision of national and organizational policies and guidance, indicating how difficult it has been to respond effectively to the challenge of fragility.

Chapter 4 summarizes the challenges encountered and lessons learned. It summarizes what has been learned about fragility and offers ideas about improving the international response. It suggests a number of ways in which various relationships—within international actors, among international actors, and between international actors and countries experiencing situations of fragility—could be strengthened and how strategies to diminish fragility and promote resilience could be made more effective. It ends with some specific ideas about how the United States might improve its management of fragility, including through international leadership.

Concluding observations and recommendations are presented at the end.

The report's purpose is to stimulate thinking and action by political leaders, public and private organizations, and citizens. The hopeful expectation is that the information and ideas presented here will be useful in advocacy for policies and programs that will help to prevent fragile situations from deteriorating into crises and conflict and will help to make societies more resilient, thereby advancing peace, security, and sustainable development.

01

Background on Violence, Development, and Fragility

Human progress over the past two centuries has been remarkable. Conflict and violence have declined as prosperity and freedom have increased. Over time, more and more people have experienced increased security, improved economic opportunities, better health, expanded access to education, and greater freedom. However, these global trends are hardly uniform. Stark differences remain among countries and regions.[1]

Steven Pinker's *The Better Angels of Our Nature* describes how pacifying, civilizing, and humanitarian trends in human behavior over centuries have influenced a pronounced decline in armed conflict and a greatly diminished societal tolerance of violence and cruelty. Pinker relates this history to a theory of how human capacities for reason, moral values, self-control, and empathy have won out over our tendencies toward predatory violence, dominance of others, revenge, sadism, and rigid ideology.

Independent research confirms that the historical trends identified by Pinker have continued in modern times. Data from numerous sources show that we have been living in the most peaceful period in human history.[2] At least until 2010, deaths in armed conflict as well as homicide rates declined in many places.[3]

---

1. See Daniel Runde, *A Tale of Two Paths: Divergence in Development* (Washington, DC: CSIS, 2017), https://csis-prod .s3.amazonaws.com/s3fs-public/publication/170227_Runde_DivergentDevelopmentLandscape_Web_0.pdf?XwSBfmA pDe9ISHvuXb8aGhuSHVcsrIbx.

2. See Max Roser, *War and Peace* (n.p.: Our World in Data, 2016), https://ourworldindata.org/war-and-peace/; Human Security Report Project, *Human Security Report 2013: The Decline in Global Violence—Evidence, Explanation, and Contestation* (Vancouver, British Columbia: Human Security Press, 2014), https://reliefweb.int/sites/reliefweb.int/files /resources/HSRP_Report_2013_140226_Web.pdf. See also Geneva Declaration on Armed Violence and Development, *Global Burden of Armed Violence 2015: Every Body Counts* (Geneva: Geneva Declaration on Armed Violence and Development, 2015), http://www.genevadeclaration.org/measurability/global-burden-of-armed-violence/global -burden-of-armed-violence-2015.html.

3. Kendra Dupuy, Håvard Mokleiv Nygård, Ida Rudolfsen, Håvard Strand, and Henrik Urdal, *Trends in Armed Conflict, 1946–2015* (Oslo: Peace Research Institute Oslo, 2016), http://files.prio.org/Publication_files/prio/Dupuy%20et%20

The past few years have seen a spike in armed conflicts and combat deaths, as well as in homicides.[4] The highly authoritative Uppsala Conflict Data Program estimated that the number of people killed in organized violence globally in 2014 exceeded 125,000, the highest since the Rwanda genocide twenty years earlier.[5] The *Global Terrorism Index 2015* reported a nine-fold increase in deaths from terrorism since 2000 (from 3,329 in 2000 to 32,685 in 2014).[6] Deficiencies in the accuracy, completeness, consistency, and timeliness of available data impede precise measurement.[7] Nevertheless, the evidence of increased violence is disturbing.

These increases are more evident in some regions and are more concentrated in some communities. Regarding homicides, the UN *Sustainable Development Goals Report 2017* indicates that in 2015, "Latin America and the Caribbean had the highest rate by far—17 times that of eastern and South-eastern Asia and 20 times the rate in Australia and New Zealand." In 2014, the Arab region, which is home to 5 percent of the world's population, accounted for two-thirds of the world's battle-related deaths; Latin America and the Caribbean, with 8 percent of global population, accounted for one-third of the world's homicides. Three-fourths of recorded acts of terrorism in every year since 2013 have occurred in just five countries (Afghanistan, Iraq, Nigeria, Syria, and Yemen), with Iraq and Nigeria accounting for more than one-half of the total.[8]

---

al%20-%20Trends%20in%20Armed%20Conflict%201946-2015,%20Conflict%20Trends%208-2016.pdf; Carlos Vilalta, *Global Trends and Projections of Homicidal Violence, 2000 to 2030* (Rio de Janeiro, Igarapé Institute, 2015), https://igarape.org.br/wp-content/uploads/2016/04/Homicide-Dispatch_2_EN_22-04-16.pdf.

4. See the collected research findings in Alexandre Marc, *Conflict and Violence in the 21st Century: Current Trends as Observed in Empirical Research and Statistics* (Washington, DC: World Bank, 2016), http://www.un.org/pga/70/wp-content/uploads/sites/10/2016/01/Conflict-and-violence-in-the-21st-century-Current-trends-as-observed-in-empirical-research-and-statistics-Mr.-Alexandre-Marc-Chief-Specialist-Fragility-Conflict-and-Violence-World-Bank-Group.pdf. See also Steven Pinker and Andrew Mack, "The World Is Not Falling Apart: Never Mind the Headlines. We've Never Lived in Such Peaceful Times," *Slate*, December 22, 2014, http://www.slate.com/articles/news_and_politics/foreigners/2014/12/the_world_is_not_falling_apart_the_trend_lines_reveal_an_increasingly_peaceful.html.

5. Erik Melander, *Organized Violence in the World 2015* (Uppsala: Uppsala Conflict Data Program, 2015), http://www.pcr.uu.se/digitalAssets/61/c_61335-l_1-k_brochure2.pdf.

6. Institute for Economics and Peace, *Global Terrorism Index 2015: Measuring and Understanding the Impact of Terrorism* (Sydney: Institute for Economics and Peace, 2015), 11, http://economicsandpeace.org/wp-content/uploads/2015/11/Global-Terrorism-Index-2015.pdf.

7. Rachel Kleinfeld, *Reducing All Violent Deaths, Everywhere: Why the Data Must Improve* (Washington, DC: Carnegie Endowment for International Peace, 2017), http://carnegieendowment.org/files/CP_297_Kleinfeld_Crime_Final_Web.pdf.

8. UNDP, *Arab Human Development Report 2016: Youth and the Prospects for Human Development in a Changing Reality* (New York: UN, 2016c), 30; OECD, *States of Fragility 2016*, 36; Institute for Economics and Peace, *Global Terrorism Index 2017: Measuring and Understanding the Impact of Terrorism* (Sydney: Institute for Economics and Peace, 2017b), 14, https://reliefweb.int/sites/reliefweb.int/files/resources/Global%20Terrorism%20Index%202017%20%284%29.pdf; World Health Organization, UN Office on Drugs and Crime, UNDP, *Global Status Report on Violence Prevention 2014* (Geneva: World Health Organization, 2014), http://www.who.int/violence_injury_prevention/violence/status_report/2014/report/report/en.

Research shows the relationship of violence to other factors associated with societal fragility, such as the rule of law and political, social, and economic stability. High concentrations of violence are often found in poor communities and in countries with high income inequality.[9]

Recent experience may constitute only a temporary aberration from the historic trend toward a less violent world. The most up-to-date studies indicate that global combat deaths declined in 2015 and 2016, that there was a slight improvement in global peace in 2016, and that terrorist attacks and fatalities from terrorism declined globally in 2015 and again in 2016. These findings are departures from the trend over the past decade.[10]

UNDERLYING CAUSES

An analysis of trends in violence and development needs to examine underlying causes. Part of the explanation of these trends is provided by research into the relationships among security, governance, and power in controlling violence and diminishing its negative impact on economic progress, human development, social interaction, and political participation.[11]

Douglass North, John Joseph Wallis, Steven Webb, and Barry Weingast provided an important perspective on these relationships in their distinction between "limited access" and "open access" societies. According to their analysis, members of a dominant coalition in a limited access order agree to respect each other's privileges as an incentive for all coalition members to avoid violence.

By contrast, in an open access order, violence is held in check through political control over military and police organizations, institutions and incentives that constrain the illegitimate use of force, and the need for broad support from economic and social interests for a political faction to retain power. North and his colleagues observed that historic transitions to open access (in what are now developed countries) have tended to occur within "relatively brief periods" of about 50 years.[12]

9. OECD, *States of Fragility 2016*, 43–46; UN, *The Sustainable Development Goals Report 2017* (New York: UN, 2017b), 50, https://unstats.un.org/sdgs/files/report/2017/TheSustainableDevelopmentGoalsReport2017.pdf. See Gary A. Haugen and Victor Boutros, *The Locust Effect: Why the End of Poverty Requires the End of Violence* (New York: Oxford University Press, 2014); Rachel Hart, "Analysis of Global Homicide Patterns" (honors thesis, University of California, Berkeley, 2015), https://www.econ.berkeley.edu/sites/default/files/HART-Honors%20Thesis.pdf.

10. International Institute for Strategic Studies, *Armed Conflict Survey 2017* (London: International Institute for Strategic Studies, 2017), 5; Institute for Economics and Peace, *Global Peace Index 2017: Measuring Peace in a Complex World* (Sydney: Institute for Economics and Peace, 2017a), 26–31, http://visionofhumanity.org/app/uploads/2017/06/GPI17-Report.pdf; Department of State, *Country Reports on Terrorism 2016* (Washington, DC: Department of State, 2017), chap. 1, https://www.state.gov/documents/organization/272488.pdf; Institute for Economics and Peace, *Global Terrorism Index 2017*, 14.

11. Tani Marilena Adams, *How Chronic Violence Affects Human Development, Social Relations, and the Practice of Citizenship* (Washington, DC: Woodrow Wilson Center, 2017), https://www.wilsoncenter.org/publication/how-chronic-violence-affects-human-development-social-relations-and-the-practice; Laura Chioda, *Stop the Violence in Latin America: A Look at Prevention from Cradle to Adulthood* (Washington, DC: World Bank, 2017); World Bank, *World Development Report 2017: Governance and the Law* (Washington, DC: World Bank, 2017), 110–129, https://openknowledge.worldbank.org/handle/10986/25880.

12. Douglass C. North, John Joseph Wallis, and Barry R. Weingast, *Violence and Social Orders: A Conceptual Framework for Interpreting Recorded Human History*, pbk. ed. (New York: Cambridge University Press, 2013). See also the

Their conclusions include several points that have much in common with views expressed by others. For example, their distinction between limited access and open access societies has something in common with Daron Acemoglu and James Robinson's distinction between societies with extractive institutions and those with inclusive institutions.[13] Their emphasis on impersonal relationships in open access orders is consistent with Soren Holmberg and Bo Rothstein's identification of impartiality as the essential factor in determining the quality of government.[14] Their observation that transitions take place over several decades is consistent with the estimates by Lant Pritchett and Frauke de Weijer of the time required (several decades for even the fastest) for states to develop basic capabilities of governance.[15]

These similarities provide evidence of some convergence in thinking. The distinguishing insight of North and his colleagues is their explicit recognition that control of violence is a principal motivation for stable social orders. From this premise, there naturally follows their conclusion that premature efforts to introduce policy and institutional reforms at variance with the logic of an existing limited access order are likely to be rejected. This is because local decisionmakers will perceive an increased risk of violence from such reforms, due to anticipated disruptions of the existing social order.[16]

The historic decline in violence discussed above has been accompanied by a global trend toward increased human well-being. The emergence of open access orders over the past two centuries has coincided with a remarkable rise in per capita income.[17] This change first became evident in Western Europe early in the nineteenth century. More recently, although there are significant differences among countries and regions, impressive strides have been taken to improve the lives of people in societies on every continent (Table 1.1).[18] As summarized by Steven Radelet, "never before have we seen such substantial improvements in income, poverty, health, education, and governance at the same time."[19]

case studies in Douglass C. North, John Joseph Wallis, Steven B. Webb, and Barry R. Weingast, *In the Shadow of Violence: Politics, Economics, and the Problems of Development* (New York: Cambridge University Press, 2013).

13. Daron Acemoglu and James Robinson, *Why Nations Fail: The Origins of Power, Prosperity, and Poverty* (New York: Crown Books, 2012).

14. Soren Holmberg and Bo Rothstein, *Good Government: The Relevance of Political Science* (Northampton, MA: Edward Elgar, 2012).

15. Lant Pritchett and Frauke de Weijer, *Fragile States: Stuck in a Capability Trap?* (Washington, DC: World Bank, 2010), http://siteresources.worldbank.org/EXTWDR2011/Resources/6406082-1283882418764/WDR_Background_Paper _Pritchett.pdf. See also World Bank, *World Development Report 2011: Conflict, Security, and Development* (Washington, DC: World Bank, 2011a), 109, https://siteresources.worldbank.org/INTWDRS/Resources/WDR2011_Full_Text.pdf.

16. See the illustration of this resistance with respect to the rule of law in Barry R. Weingast, *Why Are Developing Countries So Resistant to the Rule of Law?* (Florence: European University Institute, 2009), http://cadmus.eui.eu /bitstream/handle/1814/11173/MWP_LS_2009_02.pdf?sequence=1&isAllowed=y.

17. Angus Maddison, *The World Economy: A Millennial Perspective* (Paris: OECD, 2001).

18. Jan Luiten Van Zanden, Joerg Baten, Marco Mira d'Ercole, Auke Rijpma, Conal Smith, and Marcel Timmer, *How Was Life? Global Well-Being since 1820* (Paris: OECD, 2014).

19. Steven Radelet, *The Great Surge: The Ascent of the Developing World* (New York: Simon and Schuster, 2015), 8. See also Angus Deaton, *The Great Escape: Health, Wealth, and the Origins of Inequality* (Princeton, NJ: Princeton University Press, 2013).

Table 1.1. Per Capita Income, 1820–2016

Region or Country	1820	1870	1913	1950	1973	1998	2016
Western Europe	1,232	1,974	3,473	4,594	11,534	17,921	39,105
Former USSR	689	943	1,488	2,834	6,058	3,893	24,026
United States	1,257	2,445	5,301	9,561	16,689	27,331	52,195
Latin America	665	698	1,511	2,554	4,531	5,795	14,318
Japan	669	737	1,387	1,926	11,439	20,413	38,240
Asia (excluding Japan)	575	543	640	635	1,231	2,936	12,842
Africa	418	444	585	852	1,365	1,368	3,440

Sources: For 1820–1998, see Maddison, *The World Economy*, 264 (1990 international $); for 2016, see World Bank Data, "GDP per Capita (Current $US)," https://data.worldbank.org/indicator/NY.GDP.PCAP.CD ?view=chart (PPP, constant 2011 $).

Of course, many factors in addition to economic growth are involved in the complex and continuing long-term development process by which countries become—and remain—more stable, just, and prosperous.[20] Over the past three decades, the international community has come to a broad consensus about the goals of development and about effective international cooperation in support of those goals.[21]

---

20. Maddison, *World Economy*, 17; Dwight A. Perkins, Steven Radelet, David L. Lindauer, and Steven A. Block, *Economics of Development* (New York: W.W. Norton & Company, 2013) 23–54; The complexity of development was eloquently captured by Amartya Sen's notion that "development is freedom" and by Mahbub ul Haq's assertion that "the basic purpose of development is to enlarge people's choices." See Sen, *Development as Freedom* (New York: Knopf, 1999), 8–10; Haq, *Reflections on Human Development* (New York: Oxford University Press, 1995); Sabina Alkire, "Human Development: Definitions, Critiques, and Related Concepts," OPHI Working Paper 36 (Oxford: University of Oxford, 2010), http://www.ophi.org.uk/wp-content/uploads/OPHI_WP36.pdf.

21. The proposal by the Development Assistance Committee of the Organization for Economic Cooperation and Development (OECD/DAC) in 1996 for a set of international development goals to clarify a broad vision of development drew upon the 1990 Jontien Conference on Education for All, the 1992 Rio de Janeiro Conference on the Environment, the 1993 Vienna Conference on Human Rights, the 1994 Cairo Conference on Population, the 1995 Beijing Conference on Women, and the 1995 Copenhagen Summit for Social Development. OECD, *Shaping the 21st Century: The Contribution of Development Co-operation* (Paris: OECD, 1996). The DAC proposal provided background for the Millennium Development Goals (MDGs), which gave operational force to the UN Millennium Declaration of 2000, UNGA Res. 55/2 (2000c). The current Sustainable Development Goals were adopted at the Sustainable Development Summit in 2015 in UNGA Res. 70/1, September 25, 2015, *Transforming Our World: The 2030 Agenda for Sustainable Development.*

The SDGs adopted in 2015 are deliberately bold. They are expressly intended to change the world by ending poverty; promoting peaceful, just, and inclusive societies; and ensuring that progress will be economically, socially, and environmentally sustainable.[22]

The SDGs are universal in their application and premised on the challenging commitment "that no-one will be left behind."[23] SDG 16 highlights the breadth of this formidable challenge in situations of fragility: "Promote peaceful and inclusive societies for sustainable development, provide access to justice for all and build effective, accountable and inclusive institutions at all levels."[24]

The targets for Goal 16 clearly were formulated with fragile situations in mind. They acknowledge the significance of reduced violence and corruption, effective and accountable institutions, inclusive and participatory decisionmaking, public access to information, and nondiscriminatory laws and policies. They call for strengthening of national institutions "to prevent violence and combat terrorism and crime."[25]

COUNTRIES IN FRAGILE SITUATIONS

The countries included on recent major listings of fragile situations account for about 20 percent of the world's population, but they are home to about 50 percent of those living in extreme poverty. The total population of countries in fragile situations and the number of their people living in extreme poverty are both increasing even as the global total of people in extreme poverty is in decline. Thus, on the present trajectory a growing number of people are being left behind.

As shown in Figure 1.1, this is leading to an ever-higher concentration of extreme poverty in fragile environments. The OECD estimates that by 2035, 80 percent of extremely poor people will live in the 56 contexts identified as fragile in 2016. It is noteworthy that these are not all poor countries; 27 are low income, 25 are lower middle income, and four are upper middle income. The number of extremely poor people in the most fragile contexts is expected to increase from 92 million in 2015 to 116 million in 2035.[26]

The association of extreme poverty with fragility is only part of the challenge. Countries with fragile environments were the least successful in making progress toward any of the targets

---

22. UN, *Transforming Our World*, Preamble, 1–2.

23. Ibid.

24. Ibid., 25. See the references to fragility and resilience in UNDP, *UNDP Support to the Implementation of Sustainable Development Goal 16* (New York: UN, 2016b), http://www.undp.org/content/dam/norway/undp-ogc/documents/16_peace_Jan15_digital.pdf.

25. Ibid., 25–26.

26. OECD, *States of Fragility 2016*, 77–83. Using a different base, the World Bank estimates that the share of extreme poor living in fragile and conflict-affected situations will increase from 17 percent of the global total in 2017 to almost 50 percent by 2030. World Bank, "Fragility, Conflict and Violence," accessed November 28, 2017, http://www.worldbank.org/en/topic/fragilityconflictviolence. The obvious implication of an increased number of the extremely poor in fragile situations is that extreme poverty will not be eliminated by 2030.

Figure 1.1. Poverty in Fragile versus Not Fragile Countries, 1990–2030

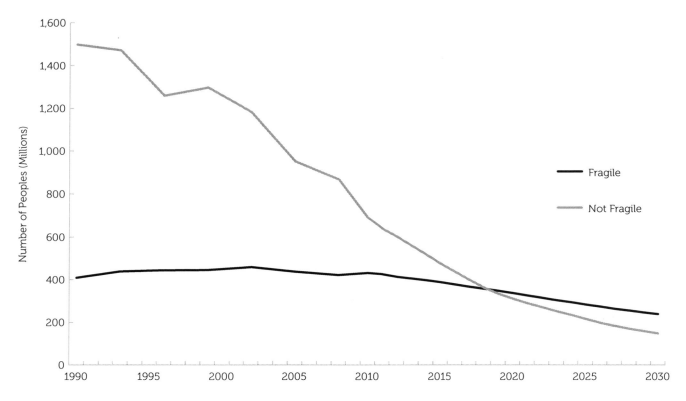

Source: Laurence Chandy, Natasha Ledlie, and Veronika Penciakova, *The Final Countdown: Prospects for Ending Extreme Poverty by 2030* (Washington, DC: Brookings Institution, 2013), 14.

established by the Millennium Development Goals.[27] Many of them have remained on the fragility lists year after year.[28] As noted above, the time needed to make the transition from a limited access to an open access society or to develop the fundamental capabilities of governance (achievements associated with economic and social progress) is measured in decades, not years, even for the best performers.

---

27. John Norris, Casey Dunning, and Annie Malknecht, *Fragile Progress: The Record of the Millennium Development Goals in States Affected by Conflict, Fragility, and Crisis* (Washington, DC: Center for American Progress and Save the Children, 2015), http://www.savethechildren.org/atf/cf/%7B9def2ebe-10ae-432c-9bd0-df91d2eba74a%7D/FRAGILESTATES -REPORT_WEB.PDF.

28. James Michel, *Beyond Aid: The Integration of Sustainable Development in a Coherent International Agenda* (Washington, DC: CSIS, 2016), 51–54, https://csis-prod.s3.amazonaws.com/s3fs-public/legacy_files/files/publication /160111_Michel_BeyondAid_Web.pdf. Many of the countries that were identified as furthest from the development goals proposed by the OECD in 1996 are included on the current lists of fragile states and situations. See the current lists in Chapter 2 of this report (Table 2.1) and the OECD's 1997 list at OECD, *Development Cooperation Report 1997: Efforts and Policies of the Members of the Development Assistance Committee* (Paris: OECD Publishing, 1998), 15, http://www.oecd-ilibrary.org/docserver/download/4398011e.pdf?expires=1505403379&id=id&accname=guest&checksum =3F86E49EEF47B78F7B9CC079D85D8C0C.

CONCLUSIONS

This chapter has presented three important realities. First, it describes how fragile situations consti-tute exceptions to global historical trends of reduced violence and increased security and well-being. Second, it shows how fragility, which accounts for a disproportionate and growing percentage of global poverty and violence, has become a potential threat to a continuation of these positive trends—a threat that is magnified by the demonstrated propensity of fragile situa-tions to give rise to negative consequences beyond national borders. Third, it has pointed out how human societies transform themselves slowly over decades, foreclosing expectations for quick results from efforts to reverse fragility. Together, these considerations provide ample reason why we need to give priority attention to ensuring effective national and international responses to this phenomenon.

02

Defining Fragility and Identifying Fragile Situations

As indicated in the Introduction, this report uses the term "fragility" as a reference to the combination of obstacles to peace, security, and sustainable development attributable to poor governance, limited institutional capability, low social cohesion, and weak legitimacy, leading to erosion of the social contract and diminished resilience.

This approach implicitly regards fragility as involving conditions that exist to some degree in a wide variety of situations. It does not draw a bright line between situations that are "fragile" and those that are not. The challenge is to understand the priority issues in particular contexts and make judgments about what needs to be done about them, and by whom.

Historically, a variety of definitions and lists of "fragile states" (sometimes with other labels) have called attention to situations and trends of broad concern. The absence of a common understanding of fragility can impede a coherent approach to dealing with these concerns. However, common understanding does not necessarily require a universally accepted definition.

DEFINING FRAGILITY

Some of the best-known examples of definitions and lists are summarized below. Useful additional material on the characteristics of fragility, definitions, and country rankings can be found in research materials and methodologies, such as those used by the organizations that sponsor the publications described below.[1]

---

1. See, for example, Claire Mcloughlin, *Topic Guide on Fragile States* (Birmingham: Governance and Social Development Resource Centre [GSDRC], 2012), http://www.gsdrc.org/docs/open/con86.pdf; Frances Stewart and Graham Brown, *Fragile States* (Oxford: Center for Research on Inequality, Human Security and Ethnicity, 2009), https://assets.publishing.service.gov.uk/media/57a08b62e5274a27b2000af7/wp51.pdf; OECD, *States of Fragility 2016*, Methodological Annex, 147–176; Carleton University Indicator Descriptions, https://carleton.ca/cifp/failed-fragile-states/indicator-descriptions/.

World Bank

The World Bank limits itself to a procedural definition: "A fragile situation is defined as having either: a) a composite World Bank, African Development Bank and Asian Development Bank Country Policy and Institutional Assessment (CPIA) rating of 3.2 or less; or b) the presence of a UN and/or regional peace-keeping or peace-building mission (e.g., African Union, European Union, NATO), with the exclusion of border monitoring operations, during the past three years."[2]

The CPIA was designed as a tool to help assess how well a low-income country's policy and institutional framework support poverty reduction, sustainable growth, and effective use of development assistance. CPIA scores are derived from a set of 16 criteria grouped in four equally weighted clusters: economic management, structural policies, policies for social inclusion and equity, and public-sector management and institutions.[3]

The World Bank publishes an annual Harmonized List of Fragile Situations, which is coordinated with the African and Asian Development Banks. This list is based on the above-quoted definition: CPIA scores for low-income countries eligible for concessional IDA assistance, plus countries with the presence of an international peacekeeping or peacebuilding mission for the last three years. For the fiscal year 2018, the Harmonized List includes 36 fragile situations, 32 based on CPIA scores and four based only on the presence of a peacekeeping or peacebuilding mission. Of the 32 situations based on CPIA scores, nine also have peacekeeping missions and seven have peace-building missions.[4]

The World Bank's definition has been the subject of periodic criticism and review. A 2013 evaluation recommended that the Bank develop a more suitable method for identifying fragile situations

---

2. World Bank, "Definition of Fragility, the IDA Exceptional Allocation Framework and the Post-Conflict Performance Indicators Framework—Q&A," http://siteresources.worldbank.org/PROJECTS/Resources/40940-1404407793868 /9611975-1404407810503/PCPI_Q&A_2013_2.pdf. The World Bank has also referred to fragile states as "countries facing particularly severe development challenges such as weak institutional capacity, poor governance, political instability, and frequently on-going violence or the legacy effects of past severe conflict." See World Bank, *Operational Approaches and Financing in Fragile States* (Washington, DC: World Bank, 2007), 2, http://siteresources .worldbank.org/IDA/Resources/IDA15FragileStates.pdf. However, this generic reference is not the Bank's formal definition.

3. The criteria are for economic management—monetary and exchange rate policies, fiscal policy, debt policy, and management; for structural policies—trade, financial sector, business regulatory environment; for social inclusion— gender equality, equity of public resource use, building human resources, social protection and labor, environmental sustainability; for public-sector management and institutions—public-sector management and institutions, property rights and rule-based governance, quality of budgetary and financial management, efficiency of revenue mobilization, quality of public administration, transparency, accountability, and corruption in the public sector. "Annex 2: IDA's Performance-Based Allocation System for IDA 18" in IDA, *Towards 2030: Investing in Growth, Resilience and Opportunity*, Report from the Executive Directors of the International Development Association to the Board of Governors (Washington, DC: World Bank, 2017), 105, http://documents.worldbank.org/curated/en/348661486654455091/pdf /112728-correct-file-PUBLIC-Rpt-from-EDs-Additions-to-IDA-Resources-2-9-17-For-Disclosure.pdf.

4. World Bank, "Harmonized List of Fragile Situations FY 18," accessed November 28, 2017, http://pubdocs.worldbank .org/en/189701503418416651/FY18FCSLIST-Final-July-2017.pdf.

in order to integrate "indicators of conflict, violence and political risks within the current system."[5] Also in 2013, a World Bank study showed an appreciation for the nuances of fragility as a dynamic continuum and a problem that includes "dysfunctional relationships across groups in society, including the relationships of different groups with the state."[6] A 2015 World Bank information note on the Harmonized List acknowledged the criticism in the 2013 evaluation and observed that "definitions built on the CPIA and peacekeeping missions can poorly account of contexts such as fragilities in middle-income countries and spatial dynamics."[7]

OECD

The OECD defines fragility as "the combination of exposure to risk and insufficient coping capacity of the state, system and/or communities to manage, absorb or mitigate those risks." The definition continues: "Fragility can lead to negative outcomes including violence, the breakdown of institutions, displacement, humanitarian crises or other emergencies."[8]

The OECD publishes an annual *States of Fragility Report*, which presents a worldwide picture of fragility. From 2005 until 2014, the OECD published a *Fragile States Report*; the change in terminology reflects an intention to look beyond quantitative measures of governance to include analysis of the interaction between risks and coping capacities.

The 2015 OECD report proposed fragility indicators for violence; universal access to justice; effective, accountable, and inclusive institutions; economic inclusion and stability; and capacities to prevent and adapt to social, economic, and environmental shocks and disasters. This approach was intended "to stimulate fresh thinking and new ideas about these dynamic states of fragility and how to better track needs, aid flows and progress in achieving the SDGs in fragile situations."[9]

The 2016 OECD report examined five dimensions of fragility: economic, environmental, political, security, and societal. For each examined country context, the new OECD fragility framework ranks each of these dimensions on a six-level scale ranging from moderate to extreme. The rankings are presented for 56 contexts with the caution that differences between closely ranked situations preclude comparison between them.[10]

5. World Bank, *World Bank Group Assistance to Low-Income Fragile and Conflict-Affected States: An Independent Evaluation* (Washington, DC: World Bank, 2014b), xli, lvi, and 159, https://ieg.worldbankgroup.org/Data/Evaluation/files /fcs_eval.pdf.

6. Alexandre Marc, Alys Wilklman, Ghazia Aslam, Michelle Rebosio, and Kanishka Balasuriya, *Societal Dynamics of Fragility: Engaging Societies in Responding to Fragile Situations* (Washington, DC: World Bank, 2013), 13, https:// openknowledge.worldbank.org/handle/10986/12222.

7. Nadia Piffaretti, Laura Ralston, and Khadija Shaikh, *Information Note: The World Bank Group's Harmonized List of Fragile Situations* (Washington, DC: World Bank, 2014), http://documents.worldbank.org/curated/en/692741468338471327 /Information-note-the-World-Banks-harmonized-list-of-fragile-situations4.

8. OECD, *States of Fragility 2016*, 22.

9. OECD, *States of Fragility 2015* (Paris: OECD, 2015), http://www.oecd-ilibrary.org/docserver/download/4315011e.pdf ?expires=1503686954&id=id&accname=guest&checksum=7B3DE0D4B9E08DB39B3DDA864E576C02.

10. OECD, *States of Fragility 2016*.

Fund for Peace

The FFP does not have its own definition of fragile states, but publishes an annual Fragile States Index which measures pressures and capabilities relating to the stability of 178 countries. The indicators are grouped into 12 factors: three cohesion indicators (security apparatus, factionalized elites, group grievance); three economic indicators (economic decline, uneven economic development, human flight and brain drain); three political indicators (state legitimacy, public services, human rights and rule of law); and three social and cross-cutting indicators (demographic pressures, refugees and internally displaced persons [IDPs], external intervention).

Countries are ranked according to their total scores into groups: very sustainable, sustainable, very stable, more stable, stable, warning, elevated warning, high warning, alert, high alert, and very high alert. Generally, countries in the last three categories (35 of them in 2017) are regarded as the most fragile.[11]

Carleton University

Carleton University in Ottawa, Canada, produces annual country indicators for foreign policy with a global fragility ranking of 198 countries. Of these, 19 countries are considered to present serious fragility conditions. The Carleton indicators cover a wide range of issues in nine major areas: history of armed conflict, governance and political instability, militarization, population heterogeneity, demographic stress, economic performance, human development, environmental stress, and international linkages. Rankings are based on "cluster scores" relating to qualities of authority, legitimacy, and capacity. The 2016 fragility report ranked states for 2015, emphasizing the links between state fragility and two major contemporary issues: climate change and refugees.[12]

Recent analysis by Carleton includes an effort to distinguish among types of state weakness on the basis of shared characteristics with respect to authority, legitimacy, and capacity. This approach goes beyond a single list that aggregates very different kinds of situations and, instead, characterizes states as brittle (susceptible to regime change), impoverished (often considered as aid darlings), and fragile (experiencing disproportionately high levels of violent internal conflict).[13]

---

11. FFP, *Fragile States Index 2017* (Washington, DC: Fund for Peace, 2017), https://reliefweb.int/sites/reliefweb.int/files/resources/951171705-Fragile-States-Index-Annual-Report-2017.pdf. See also the FFP's 2014 Conflict Assessment System Tool (CAST) methodology set forth in its *CAST Conflict Assessment Framework Manual* (Washington, DC: Fund for Peace, 2014), http://library.fundforpeace.org/library/cfsir1418-castmanual2014-english-03a.pdf, and its 2015 analysis of country performance over time, *The World in 2015: Country-by-Country Trend Analysis* (Washington, DC: Fund for Peace, 2015), http://library.fundforpeace.org/blog-20150620-countrytrends.

12. David Carment, Simon Langlois-Bertrand, and Yiagadeesen Samy, *Assessing State Fragility, with a Focus on Climate Change and Refugees* (Ottawa: Carleton University, 2016), http://www4.carleton.ca/cifp/app/serve.php/1530.pdf.

13. Peter Tikuisis and David Carment, *Categorization of States beyond Strong and Weak* (Ottawa: Carleton University, 2017), https://carleton.ca/cifp/wp-content/uploads/1549.pdf.

USAID

USAID describes fragility as referring to "the extent to which state-society relations fail to produce outcomes that are considered to be effective and legitimate."[14] The agency maintains an unpublished alert list of fragile situations.

USAID seeks to distinguish between fragile states that are "vulnerable" and those that are "in crisis." It describes those categories as follows in its 2005 strategy:

> USAID is using *vulnerable* to refer to those states unable or unwilling to adequately assure the provision of security and basic services to significant portions of their populations and where the legitimacy of the government is in question. This includes states that are failing or recovering from crisis.

> USAID is using *crisis* to refer to those states where the central government does not exert effective control over its own territory or is unable or unwilling to assure the provision of vital services to significant parts of its territory, where legitimacy of the government is weak or nonexistent, and where violent conflict is a reality or a great risk.[15]

Incidental to its strategy, USAID also published proposed indicators and a methodology for measuring political, security, economic, and social dimensions of state effectiveness and legitimacy, as well as a supplemental set of indicators. The USAID analytical model establishes a set of desired outcomes for those four dimensions and provides a menu of 34 indicators to assess individual situations.[16]

Other Organizations

The UNDP, while acknowledging the absence of a consensus definition, characterizes fragility as "not a fixed state, but rather a continuum" and regards fragile contexts as including "those countries and territories experiencing armed conflict, emerging from armed conflict, or affected by acute political, social, and economic vulnerability, and susceptible to chronic forms of organized criminal violence."[17]

The g7+ group, made up of 20 states that have experienced conflict and fragility, has been the leader in developing the New Deal approach to fragility, discussed in Chapter 3. The group has

---

14. USAID, *Ending Extreme Poverty in Fragile Contexts* (Washington, DC: USAID, 2014), 2, http://pdf.usaid.gov/pdf _docs/pnaec864.pdf.

15. USAID, *Fragile States Strategy* (Washington, DC: USAID, 2005a), 1, http://pdf.usaid.gov/pdf_docs/PDACA999 .pdf.

16. USAID, *Measuring Fragility: Indicators and Methods for Rating State Performance* (Washington, DC: USAID, 2005b), http://pdf.usaid.gov/pdf_docs/Pnadd462.pdf; USAID, *Fragile States Indicators: A Supplement to the Country Analytical Template* (Washington, DC: USAID, 2005c), http://pdf.usaid.gov/pdf_docs/Pnadg262.pdf.

17. Robert Muggah, Timothy D. Sisk, Eugenia Piza-Lopez, Jago Salmon, and Patrick Keuleers, *Governance for Peace: Securing the Social Contract* (New York: UNDP, 2012), 16–19, http://www.undp.org/content/undp/en/home/library page/crisis-prevention-and-recovery/governance_for_peacesecuringthesocialcontract.html.

adopted a definition intended to be sufficiently broad to capture the diversity of its members' experiences. Countries are free to identify their own particular weaknesses and adopt their own terminology.

The g7+ definition is "intended as a marker to make clear how we perceive the challenges we face, but is not a binding prescription." It provides the following:

> A state of fragility can be understood as a period of time during nationhood when sustainable socio-economic development requires greater emphasis on complementary peacebuilding and statebuilding activities such as building inclusive political settlements, security, justice, jobs, good management of resources, and accountable and fair service delivery.[18]

The Fragility Study Group, organized in 2016 by the leaders of the Carnegie Endowment for International Peace, Center for a New American Security, and U.S. Institute of Peace, defines fragility as "the absence or breakdown of a social contract between people and their government. Fragile states suffer from deficits of institutional capacity and political legitimacy that increase the risk of instability and violent conflict and sap the state of its resilience to disruptive shocks."[19] The study group has proposed recommendations for U.S. policy, discussed in Chapter 4, and has produced a wealth of analytical research.[20]

The Asian Development Bank (ADB) developed a distinctive fragility index in 2014, addressing economic, state (authority, legitimacy, capacity, and effectiveness), conflict and justice, and security and peace dimensions of fragility, as well as considerations of environmental stability and world risk. The index defines fragility in terms of "the state's failure to perform its function effectively and provide basic social services such as health, education, security; incapacity to uphold the rule of law; and failure to provide sustainable sources of income for the population to get out of poverty."[21]

DFID adopted a strategy for working more effectively in fragile states in 2005. DFID's working definition covered those countries "where the government cannot or will not deliver core functions to the majority of its people, including the poor." Those core functions are described as including "territorial control, safety and security, capacity to manage public resources, delivery of basic services, and the ability to protect and support the ways in which the poorest people sustain themselves." It also described features of state capacity and willingness with respect to state authority for safety and security, effective political power, economic management, and

---

18. g7+, *Note on the Fragility Spectrum* (n.p.: g7+, 2015), 1, http://www.g7plus.org/sites/default/files/resources/g7%2B%2BEnglish%2BFS%2BNote%2BDesign.pdf.

19. William Burns, Michèle Flournoy, and Nancy Lindborg, *U.S. Leadership and the Challenge of State Fragility: Fragility Study Group Report* (Washington, DC: Carnegie Endowment for International Peace, Center for a New American Security, U.S. Institute of Peace, 2016), http://www.usip.org/fragilityreport.

20. See the policy briefs collected at U.S. Institute of Peace, "Policy Briefs: U.S. Leadership and the Challenge of State Fragility," 2016, http://www.usip.org/fragilitypolicybriefs.

21. ADB, *Fragility Index for a Differentiated Approach* (Manila: ADB, 2014), https://www.adb.org/sites/default/files/publication/42814/fragility-index-differentiated-approach-fcas.pdf.

administrative capacity to deliver services. The strategy included a "proxy list" of fragile states, based on World Bank CPIA scores.[22]

The Center for Strategic Peace publishes a State Fragility Index and Matrix which ranks countries by reference to their effectiveness and legitimacy concerning security, political, economic, and social matters (the same factors used by USAID in its analytical matrix) as well as indicators for armed conflict, regime type, and net oil production or consumption. The analysis relies on a large number of indicators. This index is not published as frequently as the others described above.[23]

The Brookings Institution published an Index of State Weakness in the Developing World in 2008. This index, prepared by Susan Rice and Stewart Patrick, defines weak states as "countries that lack the essential capacity and/or will to fulfill four sets of critical government responsibilities: fostering an environment conducive to sustainable and equitable economic growth; establishing and maintaining legitimate, transparent, and accountable political institutions; securing their populations from violent conflict and controlling their territory; and meeting the basic human needs of their population."[24]

The Brookings Index ranked 141 developing countries according to each state's performance in delivering on economic, political, security, and social welfare dimensions, providing a snapshot in time of relative effectiveness. The authors intended to provide policymakers with a new tool to help them understand the unique dynamics and drivers of performance in particular states and to help them tailor and target their policy interventions. This index has not been updated.

A number of other measures of fragility are described in an appendix to the OECD 2016 *States of Fragility Report*.[25] Table 2.1 compares four lists that were updated in 2016 and 2017.

MEASURING FRAGILITY

Methodologies for measuring fragility are numerous. They all involve a large number of factors and indicators. For example, the 12 factors considered by the FFP Fragile States Index 2017 involve 48 subindicators. The OECD uses 50 indicators to measure risks and coping capabilities with respect to its five dimensions of fragility. The g7+ Fragility Spectrum examines movement toward each of five peacekeeping and statebuilding goals through five stages of progress from crisis to resilience. To take the goal of inclusive politics as an example, the spectrum calls for attention to a total of 35 indicators covering issues of political settlement, political processes and institutions, and social relationships.

All the definitions and analytical models consider similar dimensions of fragility: economic, political, security, and societal. Some also consider the environmental dimension, and some highlight

22. DFID, *Why We Need to Work More Effectively in Fragile States* (London: DFID, 2005).

23. Monty G. Marshall and Gabrielle Elzinga Marshall, *State Fragility Index and Matrix 2015* (Vienna, VA: Center for Systemic Peace, 2016), http://www.systemicpeace.org/inscr/SFImatrix2015c.pdf.

24. Susan Rice and Stewart Patrick, *Index of State Weakness in the Developing World* (Washington, DC: Brookings Institution, 2008).

25. OECD, *States of Fragility 2016*, "Existing Measures of Fragility," 147–149.

Table 2.1. Selected Partial Lists of Fragile Countries and Situations

FFP Fragile States Index, 2017	OECD *States of Fragility* 2016	Carleton Univ. 2016 Country Indicators	World Bank Harmonized List FY2018
South Sudan	Somalia	South Sudan	*IBRD-PK or PB:*
Somalia	South Sudan	Somalia	Iraq
Central African Republic	Central African Republic	Central African Republic	Lebanon
Yemen	DR Congo	Yemen	Libya
Syria	Yemen	Sudan	West Bank–Gaza
Sudan	Sudan	Afghanistan	
DR Congo	Eritrea	DR Congo	*CPIA-IDA:*
Chad	Afghanistan	Chad	Afghanistan
Afghanistan	Chad	Iraq	Burundi
Iraq	Ethiopia	Syria	Central African Republic
Haiti	Burundi	Ethiopia	Chad
Guinea	Haiti	Eritrea	Comoros
Zimbabwe	Syria	Burundi	Congo Republic
Nigeria	Iraq	Nigeria	Cote d'Ivoire
Ethiopia	Mali	Guinea	DR Congo
Guinea Bissau	Guinea	Mali	Djibouti
Burundi	Niger	Uganda	Eritrea
Pakistan	West Bank–Gaza	West Bank–Gaza	Gambia
Eritrea	Myanmar	Pakistan	Guinea-Bissau
Niger	Kenya	Guinea Bissau	Haiti

(continued)

Table 2.1. (continued)

FFP Fragile States Index, 2017	OECD *States of Fragility* 2016	Carleton Univ. 2016 Country Indicators	World Bank Harmonized List FY2018
Cote d'Ivoire	Zimbabwe	Niger	Kiribati
Kenya	Nigeria	Liberia	Kosovo
Libya	Mozambique	Haiti	Liberia
Uganda	Uganda	Cameroon	Mali
Myanmar	Guinea Bissau	Zimbabwe	Marshall Islands
Cameroon	Liberia	Kenya	Micronesia
Liberia	Pakistan	Congo	Mozambique
Mauritania	Mauritania	Gambia	Myanmar
Congo Republic	Gambia	Angola	Papua New Guinea
North Korea	Guatemala	Djibouti	Sierra Leone
Mali	North Korea	Myanmar	Solomon Islands
Angola	Angola	Tajikistan	Somalia
Nepal	Sierra Leone	Mauritania	South Sudan
Rwanda	Honduras	Comoros	Sudan
Timor-Leste	Tanzania	Libya	Syria
Egypt	Venezuela	Egypt	Togo
Gambia	Papua New Guinea	Mozambique	Tuvalu
Sierra Leone	Madagascar	North Korea	Yemen
Bangladesh	Congo Republic	Cote d'Ivoire	Zimbabwe (Blend)

Note: FFP, OECD, and Carleton University entries are in descending order of fragility. World Bank entries are in two groups in alphabetical order. In the World Bank Harmonized List, reference to IBRD means International Bank for Reconstruction and Development; reference to PK or PB means peacekeeping or peace-building mission.

particular aspects of the principal dimensions, such as justice (g7+), territorial control (DFID and Brookings), or population heterogeneity (Carleton). As shown in Table 2.1, while differing in specifics, the various definitions produce largely similar results.[26]

They also all involve deterioration of the social contract due to poor governance, inadequate institutions, low social cohesion, and weak legitimacy, resulting in diminished societal resilience. The measurement systems show that fragility can be an issue of varying degrees of severity and that severity can vary in different dimensions and at different times.

There are questions about these methodologies. For example, the World Bank's criteria for its Harmonized List include non-IDA-eligible countries only if they have peacekeeping or peacebuilding missions. Thus, the list includes Iraq, Lebanon, Libya, and West Bank–Gaza but leaves out such obvious examples of fragility as Nigeria and Pakistan. While there is a great deal of similarity among the various lists, the diversity among the situations (including at the subnational level) in the countries on all these lists is striking. One review concluded that "examination of their theoretical underpinnings lends support to the critical view that most existing approaches are undermined by a lack of solid theoretical foundations, which leads to confusion between causes, symptoms and outcomes of state fragility."[27] There are also questions about the data that provide the basis for measurement of all the factors and indicators addressed. The international community has recognized the need for a "data revolution," and has agreed in the SDGs on an explicit target for helping developing countries "to increase significantly the availability of high-quality, timely and reliable data."[28] Many countries experiencing situations of fragility face limitations on their ability to make knowledge-based decisions and report accurately about their needs and performance. Poor-quality data can thus influence both the reality and perceptions of fragility.[29]

While most of the definitions and indices tend to emphasize the performance of governments, it is important to bear in mind, as highlighted in one World Bank report, that fragility can also be understood as a problem "of dysfunctional relationships across groups in society, including the relationships of different groups with the state."[30] This is a reminder that fragility, as an indication

---

26. See Maite Reece, "Measuring Fragile States: Are the Rankings Really Different?" (The Hague: Netherlands Institute of International Relations, 2017), https://www.clingendael.org/pub/2017/monitor2017/crises_fragile_states/pdf/crises _fragile_states_appendix.pdf. This analysis is an appendix to Kars de Bruijne, *Crises: Fragile States; Thematic Study, Clingendael Strategic Monitor 2017* (The Hague: Netherlands Institute of International Relations, 2017), https://www .clingendael.org/sites/default/files/pdfs/clingendael_strategic_monitor_2017_crises_fragile_states.pdf.

27. Ines A. Ferreira, "Defining and Measuring State Fragility: A New Proposal" (paper presented at the Annual Bank Conference on Africa, Berkeley, CA, 2015), http://cega.berkeley.edu/assets/miscellaneous_files/109_-_ABCA_2015 _Ines_Ferreira_Defining_and_measuring_state_fragility__A_new_proposal_May15.pdf. The cited article includes thoughtful charts comparing existing definitions and measurement systems.

28. UN, *Transforming Our World*, 27. See "Knowledge Accumulation, Sharing, and Coordination," in Michel, *Beyond Aid*, 43–51.

29. See, for example, "Good Enough Data: The Practicality of Imperfection," in *Managing State Fragility: Conflict, Quantification and Power*, by Isabel Rocha de Siqueira (New York: Routledge, 2017), 119–124.

30. Marc et al., *Societal Dynamics of Fragility*. See also the research materials available on the website of the Action for Empowerment and Accountability Research Consortium, https://www.ids.ac.uk/idsresearch/action-for-empowerment -and-accountability.

of deterioration in the social contract, needs to be examined with respect to both governmental and societal impediments. That same report also reminds that fragility should be conceptualized as a continuum with states moving between conflict and resiliency "as they respond to shocks or opportunities."

The many variables among fragile situations suggest that it is better to base approaches to fragile situations on the facts of each individual case rather than trying to divide countries facing similar challenges between categories of "fragile" and "not fragile" situations. Moreover, the branding of some countries as "fragile" is likely to produce a defensive reaction that can impede productive collaboration.[31]

The trend is to recognize that there is what the g7+ calls a "fragility spectrum" and the UNDP (and others) calls a "continuum." The effort by the OECD to transition from a list of fragile states to an analysis of the economic, environmental, political, security, and societal dimensions of fragility is a commendable example. However, the OECD fragility framework is still evolving to move beyond what, so far, is a list that appears very similar to earlier OECD lists of fragile states.

Beyond the question of particular methodologies and indicators, the very concept of ranking states by reference to perceptions of their fragility has been questioned on the ground that it appears to regard fragility as a deviation from an idealized norm. It has been argued that such a perception bundles development, governance, and fragility issues in ways that may incentivize or even purport to justify more-intense international intervention. In this regard, it has been suggested that applying the "fragile" or "failing" label only to "poor or marginal countries" reflects a selective erosion of sovereignty.[32]

These formulae can be useful in an early warning system to help identify situations that warrant attention. However, they do not provide much guidance about what should be done or by whom. As discussed below, early warning systems have become very sophisticated. A basic problem is that they are not always well connected to timely and effective responses.

EARLY WARNING AND EARLY RESPONSE

In addition to the various indices, which are intended to identify fragile situations on the basis of recent events and trends, there has been a long-standing interest in more ambitious approaches to identifying situations in danger of conflict or other serious deterioration with a view to mounting a timely response that might prevent a crisis.

31. In the Democratic Republic of the Congo, "many leaders objected to the 'fragile state' branding," in initial discussion of the New Deal framework. Sarah Hearn, *Independent Review of the New Deal for Engagement in Fragile States* (New York: New York University Center on International Cooperation, 2016), 39. It has been suggested that a better label would be "priority strategy countries," in part because "many countries currently believe being labeled as fragile results in less access to funding, not more." Norris et al., *Fragile Progress*, 4.

32. Nehal Bhuta, "Measuring Stateness, Ranking Political Orders: Indices of State Fragility and State Failure," in *Ranking the World: Grading States as a Tool of Global Governance*, ed. Alexander Cooley and Jack Snyder (Cambridge: Cambridge University Press, 2015), 85–111; Charles Call, "Beyond the 'Failed State': Toward Conceptual Alternatives," *European Journal of International Relations* 17, no. 2 (2010): 304.

A number of early warning systems, primarily focused on conflict prevention, have been developed over the years. They have evolved as threats to security and stability have changed. Major events, including the atrocities in Bosnia and Rwanda in the 1990s, the September 11, 2001, terrorist attacks on the United States, and the surprisingly broad and vehement Arab Spring in 2011, have influenced the emergence of a broad consensus on the elements of a "good" early warning system.

Several analyses describe a good system as one that has the following elements:

- It is based close to the ground or has strong, field-based networks of monitors;
- It uses multiple sources of information and both quantitative and qualitative analytical methods;
- It capitalizes on appropriate communications and information technology;
- It provides regular reports and updates on conflict dynamics to key national and international stakeholders; and
- It has a strong link to responders or response mechanisms.[33]

Early warning mechanisms have been developed by governments, multilateral organizations, businesses, and nongovernmental organizations. Some rely on open-source information; others include analysis of sensitive intelligence information.

An interesting hybrid model, the Political Instability Task Force (formerly the State Failure Task Force), brought together distinguished representatives of academia using open-source data in a project financed by the U.S. Central Intelligence Agency. The task force collected an enormous amount of data and identified key indicators of instability which have been shown to have substantial predictive capability.[34]

Increasingly, as in the case of humanitarian early warning systems, modern technology plays an important role.[35] A part of that role is to increase the participation of communities and civil society in generating information. However, as one study cautions, "the effectiveness of these

33. David Nyheim, *Preventing Violence, War and State Collapse: The Future of Conflict Early Warning and Response* (Paris: OECD, 2009), https://www.oecd.org/dac/conflict-fragility-resilience/docs/preventing%20violence%20war%20 and%20state%20collapse.pdf. See also Brigitte Rohwerder, *Conflict Early Warning and Early Response*, Helpdesk Research Report, Institute of Development Studies (Birmingham: Governance and Social Development Research Centre [GSDRC], 2015), http://www.gsdrc.org/docs/open/hdq1195.pdf.

34. See Jack A. Goldstone, Robert H. Bates, David L. Epstein, Ted Robert Gurr, Michael B. Lustik, Monty G. Marshall, Jay Ulfelder, and Mark Woodward, "A Global Model for Forecasting Political Instability," *American Journal of Political Science* 54, no. 1 (2010): 190–208, https://sites.duke.edu/niou/files/2011/06/goldstone-bates-etal.pdf; Jack A. Goldstone, Ted Robert Gurr, Barbara Harff, Marc A. Levy, Monty G. Marshall, Robert H. Bates, David L. Epstein, et al., *State Failure Task Force Report: Phase III Findings* (2000), http://www.raulzelik.net/images/rztextarchiv/uniseminare/statefailure%20task%20force.pdf.

35. See Andrew Albertson and Ashley Moran, *Untangling the Complexity of Fragile States* (Washington, DC: Truman Center, 2017), 5–6, http://trumancenter.org/wp-content/uploads/2017/03/Untangling-the-Complexity-of-Fragile -States.pdf; J. Eli Margolis, "Following Trends and Triggers: Estimating State Instability," *Studies in Intelligence* 56, no. 1 (2012): 13–24, https://www.cia.gov/library/center-for-the-study-of-intelligence/csi-publications/csi-studies/studies/vol.-56 -no.-1/pdfs-vol-56.-no.1/Estimating%20State%20Instability%20-Extracts-Mar12-20Apr12.pdf. For examples of the uses of advanced technology, see Junwei Liang, Susanne Burger, Alex Hauptmann, and Jay D. Aronson, *Video Syn- chronization and Sound Search for Human Rights Documentation and Conflict Monitoring* (Pittsburg: Carnegie Mellon University, 2016), https://www.cmu.edu/chrs/documents/Video-Synchronization-Technical-Report.pdf. See also the

technologies continues to be undermined by the lack of connection between warning and response, although the greater involvement of affected communities and civil society is promising."[36]

INNOVATIVE APPROACHES FOR MANAGING FRAGILITY

A number of thoughtful scholars and practitioners have proposed creative ideas that can help to shape practical strategies for managing fragility based on the facts of each situation.

Pauline Baker has developed a model to examine key strengths and vulnerabilities that influence a country's situation along the continuum from crisis to resilience. The factors she found to determine a country situation include political legitimacy, uneven economic conditions, demographic pressures, the security apparatus, human rights and the rule of law, public services, group grievances, and economic decline.

Applying this analysis to a large sample of country experiences, Baker found that a state's decline with high risk of conflict was largely driven by three critical factors: the loss of political legitimacy, growing group grievance, and poor macroeconomic performance. The process of recovery was likely to be guided by the interaction among six factors: improved political legitimacy, better public services, decreased demographic pressures, reduced inequality, good macroeconomic growth, and respect for human rights and the rule of law.[37]

The implication of her findings is that it is advisable to rely on country-specific, in-depth, participatory assessments, with follow-on actions concentrated on a few identified issues of central importance. Such a focused approach would be more manageable than trying to do too many things at once, and it would seem likely to be more effective. Indeed, an adequate alert list might be produced by tracking only a relatively small number of key factors that have been found to be significant contributors to fragility.

In economic growth studies, the Hausmann-Rodrik-Velasco approach recommends identifying and addressing one or two binding constraints to growth. This model has achieved success in places where more comprehensive approaches have floundered in the face of limited capabilities.[38] A similar concentration on a few key priorities would seem a good starting point for strategies to arrest and reverse fragility. Progress in initial areas of concentration could help to gain valuable experience and build confidence and momentum, thereby creating an improved environment for an expanded reform agenda.

PeaceTech Lab website, http://www.peacetechlab.org. For comparison with a humanitarian early warning system, see the Famine Early Warning System Network website, https://www.fews.net.

36. Phuong N. Pham and Patrick Vinck, "Technology, Conflict, Early Warning Systems, Public Health, and Human Rights," *Health and Human Rights* 14, no. 2 (2012): 106–117, at 115, https://cdn2.sph.harvard.edu/wp-content/uploads/sites/13/2013/06/Pham-FINAL2.pdf.

37. Pauline H. Baker, *Reframing State Fragility and Resilience: The Way Forward* (Washington, DC: Creative Associates International, 2017), 4–5, http://www.creativeassociatesinternational.com/wp-content/uploads/2017/02/Reframing_Way_Foward.pdf. Dr. Baker is senior governance adviser at Creative Associates and is president emeritus of the FFP.

38. Ricardo Hausmann, Dani Rodrik, and Andrés Velasco, "Getting the Diagnosis Right," *Finance and Development* 43, no. 1 (2006).

Michael Crosswell, who has played a major role in USAID in analyzing the concept of fragility, has suggested another useful distinction. He has observed that many studies attribute government shortcomings to *either* insufficient political will *or* insufficient capacity, but do not always take the next step to assess which of these two causes is more relevant in a particular context. Crosswell's analysis suggests that some aspects of governance are more resource and capacity dependent than others, noting that correlations of Worldwide Governance Indicators[39] with per capita income vary from weak (for voice and accountability) to significant (for government effectiveness and regulatory quality). He concludes that in countries where low scores on governance indicators reflect mainly limited resources and capacity, international assistance can help overcome those limitations to good effect. On the other hand, where low scores are primarily due to limited political commitment, he suggests that international assistance to help strengthen governance capabilities is not a sufficient response and is likely to be futile in the absence of effective measures to address the underlying political context.[40]

This analysis is consistent with the observation by Daron Acemoglu that the need for economic policy reform is "not because country governments do not understand basic economic principles."[41] Rather, political economy constraints may create incentives that conflict with reform initiatives. Thus, recommendations to promote "good economics" (or "good governance") may be "bad politics." It is also consistent with the caution expressed by North, Wallis, Webb, and Weingast that institutional reforms need to be introduced in a manner consistent with the logic and political incentives operating in the particular social order.[42]

In the same vein, a 2015 analysis by Ines Ferreria builds on work by Timothy Besley and Torsten Persson to suggest that fragility can be defined entirely by reference to political conditions. Her definition assumes that there is state fragility when the country exhibits one or both of two symptoms: (i) "state ineffectiveness in enforcing contracts, protecting property, providing public goods

39. The Worldwide Governance Indicators track the performance of more than 200 countries with respect to voice and accountability, political stability and absence of violence, government effectiveness, regulatory quality, rule of law, and control of corruption. See the website at http://info.worldbank.org/governance/wgi/#home.

40. Michael J. Crosswell, *Governance, Development and Foreign Aid Policy* (Oxford: 2010 Oxford Business & Economics Conference Program), http://pdf.usaid.gov/pdf_docs/PBAAD523.pdf.

41. Daron Acemoglu, "Interactions between Governance and Growth," in *Governance, Growth, and Development Decision-Making*, ed. Douglass North, Daron Acemoglu, Francis Fukuyama, and Dani Rodrik (Washington, DC: World Bank, 2008), 4, http://siteresources.worldbank.org/EXTPUBLICSECTORANDGOVERNANCE/Resources/governanceand growth.pdf.

42. Douglass C. North, John Joseph Wallis, Steven B. Webb, and Barry R. Weingast, *Limited Access Orders in the Developing World: A New Approach to the Problems of Development* (Washington, DC: World Bank, 2007), 41, https://openknowledge.worldbank.org/bitstream/handle/10986/7341/WPS4359.pdf?sequence=1&isAllowed=y, notes:

> Typical recommendations aim to introduce unmodified elements of open access orders into developing societies. These elements—property rights, the market, institutions of the rule of law, and democracy—can fail when inserted into limited access orders without taking account of the problem of the endemic distribution of the potential for violence. . . . Our model predicts that they will yield the expected benefits only if consistent with the logic of limited access in the actual country circumstance.

and raising revenues" or (ii) "political violence either in the form of repression or civil conflict," or when both these pathologies are present at the same time.[43]

The World Bank's 2017 *World Development Report* (*WDR*) takes up this theme by suggesting that changes in policy are often inhibited by asymmetries in the balance of power among key actors, often manifested by exclusion of some from the bargaining arena, capture by influential groups, and clientelism that provides benefits in exchange for political support.

According to the 2017 *WDR* analysis, changes in contestability, incentives, and preferences and beliefs are needed to correct these power asymmetries. Further, the key drivers of change needed to improve prospects for reform are elite bargains, citizen engagement, and international influence. The *WDR* also notes that engagement in the political aspects of reform is "something that many development organizations have not yet decided they are willing to do."[44]

This analysis confirms that national and international actors alike need to look beyond support for capacity building (and, more generally, beyond the limitations of aid relationships) in order to address issues of participation, political commitment, incentives, and preferences and beliefs in situations where improved governance is central to addressing fragility. The complexity of this challenge is illustrated by reports of the difficulties—beyond technical capacity—experienced in trying to promote the adoption of essential values, such as participation and accountability, at the local level in fragile situations.[45]

Charles Call provides an additional distinctive approach focused on key issues that underlie fragility. Drawing on his broad experience as a practitioner and extensive research, he questions the value of labeling countries as "fragile" or "failing." Call recommends an alternative approach based on consideration of the three gaps that the Commission on Weak States had identified in 2004 as characteristics that are typical of fragile situations:

- A capacity gap, where the institutions of a state are incapable of delivering essential public goods and services to the population.

- A security gap, where a state does not provide minimal levels of security in the face of organized armed groups.

- A legitimacy gap, where a significant population of elites and society reject the rules regulating the exercise of power and the accumulation and distribution of wealth.[46]

43. Ines A. Ferreria, "Defining and Measuring State Fragility: A New Proposal" (paper presented at the Annual Bank Conference on Africa, Berkeley, CA, 2015), http://cega.berkeley.edu/assets/miscellaneous_files/109_-_ABCA_2015 _Ines_Ferreira_Defining_and_measuring_state_fragility__A_new_proposal_May15.pdf. See also Timothy Besley and Torsten Persson, *Fragile States and Development Policy* (London: London School of Economics and Political Science, 2011b), http://sticerd.lse.ac.uk/dps/eopp/eopp22.pdf.

44. World Bank, *World Development Report 2017*, 6–13, 271.

45. See, for example, Rosemary McGee and Celestine Kroesschell, *Local Accountabilities in Fragile Contexts: Experiences from Nepal, Bangladesh and Mozambique* (Brighton: Institute of Development Studies, 2013), http://www.ids.ac .uk/files/dmfile/Wp422.pdf.

46. Commission on Weak States and U.S. National Security, *On the Brink: Weak States and the U.S. National Security* (Washington, DC: Center for Global Development, 2004), 14–16. See also UNDP, *Human Development Report 2005* (New York: UNDP, 2005), 162–163, http://hdr.undp.org/sites/default/files/reports/266/hdr05_complete.pdf.

An important feature of Call's analysis is that the international response to these gaps can create policy conflicts. In this regard, the normal response to a capacity gap is to assist the government. The response to a legitimacy gap is often to assist counterweights to the government. And a security gap, especially in a postconflict situation, may lead to assistance to both the government and its opponents in furtherance of reconciliation. "Good policy," Call concludes, "requires knowing how and when to balance the need to reassure former enemies against the need for improved capacity, the need to foster legitimate rule with the short-term security concerns or long-term capacity requirements."[47]

It is noteworthy that Call's analysis of gaps in capacity, security, and legitimacy is presented as an alternative to designating countries as "fragile" and "not fragile." At the same time, as discussed above, Carleton University ranks country fragility by reference to scores relating to authority, legitimacy, and capacity gaps. Thus, a similar analytical approach can be directed either to a country-specific strategy or to a comparative ranking that may call attention to the need for action with respect to a particular country.

Similarly, a thoughtful analysis by J. Eli Margolis describes three trends that influence stability as authority, resilience, and legitimacy. Margolis asserts that as state capacity with respect to each of these trends declines, the state becomes increasingly vulnerable to an event that can "trigger" a crisis of instability or conflict. (The lower a state's authority, resilience, and legitimacy, the more it becomes vulnerable to being thrown into chaos by a relatively weak trigger.) Margolis examines how context-specific analysis using this framework can help to shape an appropriate response.[48]

CONCLUSIONS

This chapter has shown that there are many definitions of fragility and many ways to identify fragile situations and assess their gravity. While there is no uniformity in these definitions and analyses, they all tend to rely on detailed methodologies and numerous indicators to produce largely similar results.

Some knowledgeable experts have drawn on the various frameworks and indicators to develop creative ideas about how international efforts might better respond to fragility by focusing on essential economic, political, societal, and security issues. These ideas merit consideration in efforts to shape more effective strategies.

---

47. Call, "Beyond the 'Failed State.'" Professor Call's gap analysis provides a basis for assessing operating environments in fragile situations and for aligning security, humanitarian, and development efforts. See also Anthony Bell, Kathryn McNabb Cochran, Melissa Dalton, Marc Frey, Alice Hunt Friend, Rebecca K. C. Hersman, and Sarah Minot, *Meeting Security Challenges in a Disordered World* (Washington, DC: CSIS, 2017), https://www.csis.org/analysis/meeting-security-challenges-disordered-world.

48. See Margolis, "Following Trends and Triggers."

03

The International Response to Fragility

The international response to the challenges of fragility has been influenced by three major concerns. One is the growing resource demands of disasters and postconflict situations. A second is that some countries are not making progress toward sustainable development and are being left behind. Third, and most influential of all, is the international shock of terrorism.

The resource demands of disasters and conflict situations became especially acute at the end of the Cold War. Declining development assistance budgets coincided with local and regional conflicts of high frequency and intensity in the 1990s (Afghanistan, Bosnia, Colombia, Rwanda, Iraq, etc.). Demands on donors to respond to these urgent situations were seen to be diverting increasingly scarce resources away from long-term efforts to address underlying causes of conflict and promote development. Improving the effectiveness of efforts to prevent conflict and to support transitions from conflict to stability and development became an increasingly important objective of development cooperation.[1]

By 1997 the World Bank had published a new framework on postconflict reconstruction[2] and the OECD Development Assistance Committee (OECD/DAC) had adopted guidelines on the role of development cooperation in conflict prevention, transitions to peace, and postconflict situations.[3]

1. See, for example, Carnegie Commission on Preventing Deadly Conflict, *Final Report: Preventing Deadly Conflict* (New York: Carnegie Corporation of New York, 1997), https://www.carnegie.org/media/filer_public/b2/0e/b20e1080 -7830-4f2b-9410-51c14171809b/ccny_report_1997_ccpdc_final.pdf; Kevin Cahill, ed., *Preventive Diplomacy: Stopping Wars before They Start* (New York: Routledge, 2000). See also the UN secretary-general's reports in 1992, *An Agenda for Peace: Preventive Diplomacy, Peacemaking, and Peacekeeping*, UNGA Res. 47/120 (1992b), http://www.un.org /documents/ga/res/47/a47r120.htm; 1994, *An Agenda for Development*, UNGA Res. 48/166 (1994), http://www.un -documents.net/a48r166.htm; and 1996, *An Agenda for Democratization*, UNGA Doc. A/51/761 (1996), http://www.un .org/fr/events/democracyday/pdf/An_agenda_for_democratization.pdf.

2. World Bank, *Post-Conflict Reconstruction: The Role of the World Bank* (Washington, DC: World Bank, 1998), http://documents.worldbank.org/curated/pt/175771468198561613/pdf/multi-page.pdf.

3. OECD, "Conflict, Peace and Development Cooperation on the Threshold of the 21st Century," in *Preventing Violent Conflict* (Paris: OECD, 2001), 77–155.

For its part, the United Nations produced in 2000 the report of the Panel on United Nations Peace Operations (Brahimi report).[4] These multilateral initiatives have evolved into the UN peacebuilding architecture,[5] the World Bank Fragility, Conflict, and Violence Program,[6] and the OECD/DAC International Network on Conflict and Fragility (INCAF).[7]

Regarding the second concern, the continuing lack of progress by some countries toward development goals, development experts have long emphasized the importance of partnership and local initiative for effective international development cooperation.[8] Experience has shown the limits of conditioning assistance upon the adoption of "appropriate" policies and institutions.[9] Likewise, selectivity in choosing partners that have already demonstrated their commitment to sound policies and effective institutions may improve prospects for sustainable progress in the selected countries. But it leaves out those countries most in need, in particular, those experiencing the greatest fragility.[10]

In the late 1990s both the World Bank and the DAC were struggling with the challenge of overcoming resistance to change in chronically weak performing countries where aid donors and local governments often did not share common objectives. Their concerns about the limited progress in these countries manifested itself in efforts to improve aid effectiveness. These efforts included initiatives on what the World Bank called "low income countries under stress" and the DAC called "difficult partnerships."[11]

4. UN, *Report of the Panel on United Nations Peace Operations*, UN Doc. A/55/305, S/2000/809 (New York: UN, 2000a), http://www.un.org/en/ga/search/view_doc.asp?symbol=A/55/305.

5. See the summary description in UN, "The United Nations Peacebuilding Architecture" (New York: UN, 2010), https://www.un.org/en/peacebuilding/pbso/pdf/pbso_architecture_flyer.pdf. See also the critical review in Sarah Hearn, Alejandra Kubitschek Bujones, and Alischa Kugel, *The United Nations "Peacebuilding Architecture": Past, Present and Future* (New York: New York University Center on International Cooperation, 2014).

6. See World Bank, "Fragility, Conflict and Violence," http://www.worldbank.org/en/topic/fragilityconflictviolence/overview#1.

7. See the OECD, "Conflict, Fragility and Resilience," http://www.oecd.org/dac/governance-peace/conflict fragilityandresilience/.

8. See, for example, Commission on International Development, *Partners in Development* (Pearson Commission) (New York: Praeger, 1969). Actual practice in implementing the partnership approach has been the subject of considerable study. See, for example, Karen Del Biondo, *The EU, the US, and Partnership in Development Cooperation: Bridging the Gap?* (Stanford, CA: Stanford Center on Democracy, Development and the Rule of Law, 2014), https://fsi.fsi .stanford.edu/sites/default/files/del_biondo_2_final.pdf.

9. Tony Killick, with Ramani Gunatilaka and Ana Marr, *Aid and the Political Economy of Policy Change* (New York: Routledge, 1998).

10. See David Dollar and Lant Pritchett, *Assessing Aid: What Works, What Doesn't, and Why* (New York: Oxford University Press, 1998), http://documents.worldbank.org/curated/en/612481468764422935/pdf/multi-page.pdf; Craig Burnside and David Dollar, *Aid, Policies, and Growth* (Washington, DC: World Bank, 2009), http://documents.worldbank .org/curated/en/698901468739531893/pdf/multi-page.pdf.

11. See World Bank, *World Bank Group Work in Low-Income Countries under Stress: A Task Force Report* (Washington, DC: World Bank, 2002), http://documents.worldbank.org/curated/en/329261468782159006/World-Bank-Group-work -in-low-income-countries-under-stress-a-task-force-report; OECD, "Working for Development in Difficult Partnerships," in *2002 Development Cooperation Report*, 153–164 (Paris: OECD, 2003), http://www.oecd-ilibrary.org/doc server/download/4303311e.pdf?expires=1506184960&id=id&accname=guest&checksum=C6CE3BE92B4EB62255710019 A100B370.

The 2005 Paris Declaration on Aid Effectiveness addressed this challenge in a section specifically directed at engaging fragile states:

> The long-term vision for international engagement in fragile states is to build legitimate, effective and resilient state and other country institutions. While the guiding principles of effective aid apply equally to fragile states, they need to be adapted to environments of weak ownership and capacity and to immediate needs for basic service delivery.[12]

The Paris Declaration's vision was confirmed in the 2008 Accra Agenda for Action, in which participants committed to take specific actions to improve effectiveness in fragile environments. These actions related to joint assessments of governance and capacity; agreement on realistic peace- and state-building objectives; demand-driven, tailored, and coordinated capacity-development support for core state functions; flexible, rapid, and long-term funding modalities; and monitoring of implementation of the OECD Principles for Good International Engagement in Fragile States and Situations.[13]

The 2011 Busan Partnership Declaration codified agreement on the principles of local ownership, a focus on results, inclusive partnerships, and mutual accountability and transparency. It also endorsed an operational framework that emphasizes strong, sustainable economic growth; a greater role for governments' own revenues and greater governmental accountability to citizens; effective state and nonstate institutions; and increased regional and global integration by developing countries. With respect to fragile states, Busan welcomed the New Deal developed by the International Dialogue on Peacebuilding and Statebuilding (discussed below), which provided a specific approach to applying the Busan principles and framework in fragile contexts.[14]

Subsequent research and experience have produced helpful refinement of the Busan principles and framework. Especially notable contributions are the problem-driven, iterative adaptation approach and the closely related Doing Development Differently Manifesto. The key judgments from this line of research and related field work are that international actors should focus on locally identified problems and work with local actors in flexible ways that embrace frequent

12. *Paris Declaration on Aid Effectiveness* (Paris: OECD, 2005), para. 37, http://www.oecd.org/dac/effectiveness/34428351.pdf.

13. *Accra Agenda for Action* (Tunis: African Development Bank, 2008), para. 21, https://www.afdb.org/fileadmin/uploads/afdb/Documents/AccraAgendaAaction-4sept2008-FINAL-ENG_16h00.pdf.

14. Busan Conference, *Busan Partnership for Effective Development Cooperation* (2011), http://www.oecd.org/development/effectiveness/49650173.pdf, paragraphs 11 (shared principles to achieve common goals), 26 (promoting sustainable development in situations of conflict and fragility), and 28 (from effective aid to cooperation for effective development). Preceding conferences included the high-level forum on aid effectiveness in Rome (2003), Paris (2005), and Accra (2008); the conferences on development finance in Monterrey (2002) and Doha (2008); the high-level event on south-south cooperation in Bogota (2010); the Dili meeting on peacebuilding and statebuilding (2010); and the global assembly of the Open Forum for CSO (civil society organization) Development Effectiveness at Istanbul (2010).

review and adaptation, build trust, empower people, and promote sustainable results.[15] These ideas have been widely endorsed, and while progress is still uneven, they are gaining acceptance in the practice of the international development community.[16]

Concerns about resource demands and the challenges of effective development cooperation, described above, were overtaken by an alarming increase in terrorist acts. A series of aircraft and embassy bombings and attacks on civilians during the 1980s and 1990s, culminating in the tragedies of September 11, 2001, made more starkly evident than ever before that fragility was more than a development issue. As it was observed at the time, "The weak and failed states emerged as a central challenge in both the fight against terrorism and the fight against poverty."[17]

The expanding number of countries affected by terrorist acts, together with massive displacement of people from their homes, has had a profound effect on how we think about fragility. While still highly concentrated, the *Global Terrorism Index 2017* reports that the number of countries experiencing at least one terrorism-related death in 2016 was higher than in any other year since data was first collected in 1970. Of the 10 countries that accounted for 85 percent of global terrorism deaths in 2016, 8 were included on the principal lists of fragile states and situations.[18] More than 65 million people were displaced from their homes at the end of 2016. Not surprisingly, the principal sources of refugees were countries on these lists.[19]

---

15. Matt Andrews, Lant Pritchett, and Michael Woolcock, *Escaping Capability Traps through Problem-Driven Iterative Adaptation*, Center for Global Development Working Paper 299 (Washington, DC: Center for Global Development, 2012), http://www.cgdev.org/sites/default/files/1426292_file_Andrews_Pritchett_Woolcock_traps_FINAL_0.pdf; Doing Development Differently, "The Manifesto," http://doingdevelopmentdifferently.com/the-ddd-manifesto.

16. See, for example, USAID, *Local Systems: A Framework for Supporting Sustained Development* (Washington, DC: USAID, 2012b), https://www.usaid.gov/policy/local-systems-framework; and USAID, Automated Directives System Chapter 201, "Program Cycle Operational Policy" (Washington, DC: USAID, 2016), https://www.usaid.gov/ads/policy/200/201. See also Sumedh Rao, *Problem-Driven Iterative Approaches and Wider Governance Reform* (Birmingham: GSDRC, 2014), http://gsdrc.org/docs/open/hdq1099.pdf.

17. Commission on Weak States and U.S. National Security, *On the Brink* foreword by Center for Global Development president Nancy Birdsall. See Gary LaFree, Laura Dugan, and Erin Miller, *Putting Terrorism in Context: Lessons from the Global Terrorism Database* (New York: Routledge, 2015).

18. Institute for Economics and Peace, *Global Terrorism Index 2017* (Sydney: Institute for Economics and Peace, 2017b), 16, 41, https://reliefweb.int/sites/reliefweb.int/files/resources/Global%20Terrorism%20Index%202017%20%284%29.pdf. The 10 countries accounting for 85 percent of deaths from terrorism in 2016 were Iraq, Afghanistan, Syria, Nigeria, Pakistan, Somalia, Turkey, Yemen, Democratic Republic of Congo, and South Sudan. See also Monty G. Marshall and Benjamin R. Cole, *Global Report 2014: Conflict, Governance, and State Fragility* (Vienna, VA: Center for Systemic Peace, 2014), 15–20, http://www.systemicpeace.org/vlibrary/GlobalReport2014.pdf; OECD, *States of Fragility 2016*, 31–67.

19. UN High Commissioner for Refugees, *Global Trends: Forced Displacement in 2016* (Geneva: UNHCR, 2017), 5, 17, http://www.unhcr.org/5943e8a34.

Fragile states were identified as a strategic risk in each of the U.S. National Security Strategies approved by Presidents Bush and Obama, and President Trump's new National Security Strategy acknowledges their potential relevance to threats to the American homeland.[20] They also feature prominently in security policy declarations of other countries.[21]

The challenges posed by fragility are inherently complex and the international community has found it difficult to respond effectively. In the long term, the transformation to a more stable and resilient society is a development process that requires continuous, iterative, problem-driven efforts with an emphasis on local commitment and capabilities. In the short term, fragility sometimes presents a security problem with a more immediate time frame and pressures for direct intervention by international actors. Some form of intervention may be necessary in a given case to maintain or restore peace, but it can also undermine local systems and disrupt the inherently endogenous process of sustainable development. Each situation is unique and efforts in each case must be adapted to the local context. Fragility has been called one of those "wicked problems" that defy both definition and solution.[22]

The complexity of the challenges to both security and development, together with the variety of fragile situations in the world, means that an effective response must involve numerous country-specific efforts by highly diverse local and international entities with differing mandates, capabilities, perspectives, cultures, expertise, staffing practices, and resources. In turn, the multiplicity of participants and situations has stimulated demands for more comprehensive and coherent whole-of-government and whole-of-society strategies.[23]

---

20. Texts of all National Security Strategy reports since 1987 are available at the website of the National Security Strategy Archive, http://nssarchive.us.

21. The 2015 UK National Security Strategy undertakes to "build stability overseas, upholding our values and focusing more of our development effort on fragile states and regions" and confirms the need for "a consolidated, whole-of-government effort, using our diplomatic, development, defence and law enforcement capabilities, as well as drawing on external expertise" (*Her Majesty's Government, National Security Strategy and Strategic Defence and Security Review 2015: A Secure and Prosperous United Kingdom* [London: Controller of Her Majesty's Stationery Office, 2015], 11, 64, www.gov.uk/government/publications). The 2016 Global Strategy for EU Foreign and Security Policy states, "We increasingly observe fragile states breaking down in violent conflict. These crises, and the unspeakable violence and human suffering to which they give rise, threaten our shared vital interests" (European Union, *Shared Vision, Common Action: A Stronger Europe—A Global Strategy for the European Union's Foreign and Security Policy* [Brussels: Publications Office of the EU, 2016], 28, http://eeas.europa.eu/archives/docs/top_stories /pdf/eugs_review_web.pdf). See also Seth Kaplan, "Weak States: When Should We Worry?," *American Interest* 12, no. 4 (2017), http://www.the-american-interest.com/2017/01/26/weak-states-when-should-we-worry; and Stewart Patrick, *Weak Links: Fragile States, Global Threats, and International Security* (New York: Oxford University Press, 2011).

22. Derick Brinkerhoff, "State Fragility and Failure as Wicked Problems: Beyond Naming and Taming," *Third World Quarterly* 35, no. 2 (2014): 138–139. See also Thomas Friedman, *Thank You for Being Late: An Optimist's Guide to Thriving in the Age of Accelerations* (New York: Farrar, Straus and Giroux, 2016), 286 (describing a "World of Disorder").

23. See, for example, Stewart Patrick, "U.S. Policy toward Fragile States: An Integrated Approach to Security and Development," in *The White House and the World: A Global Development Agenda for the Next U.S. President*, ed. Nancy Birdsall (Washington, DC: Center for Global Development, 2008), 327–353; Andrew Albertson and Ashley Moran, *A Call for a New Strategic Approach to Fragile States* (Washington, DC: Truman Center, 2016), http://truman center.org/wp-content/uploads/2011/07/A-Call-for-a-New-Strategic-Approach-to-Fragile-States.pdf; Stefani Weiss,

Managing Fragility and Promoting Resilience

What the development community considers the challenge of overcoming fragility, the security community describes as a challenge of stabilization. These are highly interdependent concepts, but they are not identical. Stability is necessary to achieve development, and it is hard to sustain stability without development. Development progress tends to be accompanied by increased stability.

All responsible national and international actors want to contribute to a stable environment of peace and opportunity. Making their respective contributions effective will require thoughtful efforts to overcome the different understandings and perspectives that impede efficient coordination and complicate the planning and implementation of coherent strategies. International actors need to find in each case the appropriate balance and division of labor for addressing issues of capacity and commitment in pursuit of shared objectives.

THE U.S. APPROACH

The United States has achieved only limited progress toward a comprehensive approach. The efforts have been oriented primarily toward fragile situations that are approaching or already have reached crisis proportions. There has been evidence of improving interagency coordination in this context.

Interagency coordination was demonstrated by the participation of nine U.S. agencies in the preparation of a general guide on counterinsurgency that was designed as a whole-of-government, whole-of-society interagency initiative. The guide was approved in January 2009 by the secretary of state, secretary of defense, and administrator of USAID.[24] In addition, an interagency group with Department of State, USAID, and Department of Defense participation produced an Interagency Conflict Assessment Framework in 2008, a tool for planning conflict prevention, contingency preparation, and response.[25] A 2016 Department of State and USAID joint strategy on countering violent extremism benefited from a broad-ranging international dialogue under U.S. and also under UN auspices.[26]

The mission of the Department of State's Bureau of Conflict and Stabilization Operations is to help the U.S. government "anticipate, prevent, and respond to conflict and promote long-term stability." The bureau monitors a large number of fragile situations, but appears to concentrate on a few

---

Hans-Joachim Spanger, and Wim van Meurs, eds., *Diplomacy, Development and Defense: A Paradigm for Policy Coherence—A Comparative Analysis of International Strategies* (Gütersloh: Verlag Bertelsmann Stiftung, 2009), describes strategies of the United States, the United Kingdom, Germany, the Netherlands, and the European Union as of 2009.

24. Department of State, Department of Defense, USAID, *U.S. Government Counterinsurgency Guide* (Washington, DC: Department of State, 2009), https://www.state.gov/documents/organization/119629.pdf.

25. Department of State, *Interagency Conflict Assessment Framework* (Washington, DC: Department of State, 2008), https://www.state.gov/documents/organization/187786.pdf.

26. Department of State and USAID, *Joint Strategy on Countering Violent Extremism* (Washington, DC: USAID, 2016), http://pdf.usaid.gov/pdf_docs/PBAAE503.pdf.

priorities, such as Burma (Myanmar), Colombia, Democratic Republic of the Congo, Yemen, and East Africa.[27] Interagency coordination is central to the bureau's work.

The Departments of State and Defense jointly manage a Global Security Contingency Fund, while the Department of State has a role in the management of the USAID Complex Crisis Fund. The latter fund relates to the implementation of the Department of State–USAID Strategic Plan, 2014–2017, which includes an objective to "prevent and respond to crises and conflict, tackle sources of fragility, and provide humanitarian assistance to those in need."[28]

USAID carries out programs in a wide range of fragile situations and also provides humanitarian assistance. It operates in conditions of violent extremism and insurgency in coordination with interagency and other partners.[29] The agency's Office of Conflict Management and Mitigation provides technical and analytical support to field missions, leads conflict assessments, and disseminates a wide variety of guidance documents. Coordination with the Department of Defense is guided by a USAID policy and facilitated by the agency's Office of Civilian-Military Cooperation.[30] Nevertheless, differences in organizational mission and culture continue to hamper shared understanding and effective collaboration in the field.[31]

The Millennium Challenge Corporation (MCC) is less directly involved in the U.S. response to fragility because its focus is on countries that have demonstrated through their performance that they are committed to good governance, economic freedom, and investments in their citizens.[32] Nevertheless, MCC has entered into compacts with several countries that are included on the published lists of fragile states, such as Liberia and Niger.[33] MCC's model of compacts to support inclusive economic growth has considerable appeal for those fragile environments where the political environment is conducive to collaboration based on country ownership and mutual accountability. However, analysts have advised caution in adapting the MCC compact model to complex fragile environments.

---

27. See the bureau's website, https://www.state.gov/j/cso, and fact sheet, https://www.state.gov/documents /organization/268795.pdf.

28. The Global Security Contingency Fund is a pilot fund-pooling initiative authorized under Section 1207 of the National Defense Authorization Act for FY 2012 (P.L. 112-81), as amended. At present, it will expire at the end of FY 2017. The Complex Crisis Fund was authorized by the Consolidated Appropriations Act for FY 2010 (P.L. 111-117). The relevant section of the Department of State–USAID Strategic Plan is Strategic Objective 2.3, 20–22, https://www.state .gov/documents/organization/223997.pdf.

29. USAID, *The Development Response to Violent Extremism and Insurgency* (Washington, DC: USAID, 2011), https:// www.usaid.gov/sites/default/files/documents/1870/VEI_Policy_Final.pdf; Department of State and USAID, *Joint Strategy on Countering Violent Extremism.* See USAID, "Working in Crises and Conflict," https://www.usaid.gov/what -we-do/working-crises-and-conflict.

30. USAID, *Policy on Cooperation with the Department of Defense* (Washington, DC: USAID, 2015), https://www.usaid .gov/sites/default/files/documents/1866/USAIDPolicyCooperationDoD.pdf. See USAID, "Office of Civilian-Military Cooperation," https://www.usaid.gov/military.

31. See G. Willian Anderson, "Bridging the Divide: How Can USAID and DoD Integrate Security and Development More Effectively in Africa?," *Fletcher Forum of World Affairs* 38, no. 1 (2014): 101–126.

32. Millennium Challenge Act of 2003, section 607(b), 22 U.S.C. 7706(b).

33. See the countries listed at MCC, "Where We Work," https://www.mcc.gov/where-we-work.

A policy brief prepared by Alicia Phillips Mandaville for the Fragility Study Group warns that the United States should be extremely selective in using compacts in fragile environments. She recommends efforts to ensure that expectations are mutually shared, that the parties are being transparent about the intended results and measures of success, that they establish realistic implementation structures with an eye toward enhancing legitimacy and capacity, and that circumstances (including security and political factors) be defined that might warrant a change or termination in U.S. engagement.[34]

John Norris has recommended that the U.S. approach to fragile situations incorporate "many elements of the model employed by . . . MCC." He would adapt the MCC model to proposed "Inclusion, Growth, and Peace Compacts" as instruments to "provide substantial, consistent, and targeted assistance aimed at developing stronger and more legitimate institutions in partner countries."

Norris would rely on interagency implementation of these compacts under the guidance of an independent bipartisan board chaired by the secretary of state. USAID would provide operational leadership and would engage the substantial field presence of the Department of State, USAID, and (where relevant) the Department of Defense. The compacts could address a broad range of economic, political, and security issues, ideally in a context of prevention rather than in a more difficult postcrisis or postconflict situation. They would involve more diplomatic and security oversight and support than is normal for MCC programs. Key points for this proposal are the logic of early engagement before situations deteriorate and the need for reliable, continued partnerships. Norris proposes a distinct set of indicators for both compact eligibility and measurement of implementation progress.[35]

Compacts based on locally owned partnerships and mutual accountability are the principal instruments for implementing the multilateral New Deal for Engagement in Fragile States, discussed below in this chapter. The compact approach clearly has much to commend it. At the same time, the difficulties encountered by the New Deal and by MCC in fragile environments certainly warrant caution as recommended by Mandaville and coordinated interagency oversight as recommended by Norris. The potential value of MCC and New Deal experience with the compact approach in U.S. efforts to diminish fragility and promote reliance is addressed in Chapter 4.

Considering the emphasis on conflict situations in U.S. practice and the substantial resources of the Department of Defense, it is understandable that there is a major military component in the U.S. response to fragility. That role is summarized in the 2016 joint doctrine on stabilization of the Joint Chiefs of Staff:

> Stability is needed when a state is under stress and cannot cope. In general, stabilization is usually the responsibility of the host nation (HN), Department of State, and the United States Agency for International Development with support by the Department of Defense (DOD) conducting stability actions as necessary. . . . Stability actions are often conducted in support of other USG

34. Alicia Phillips Mandaville, *Applying the Compact Model of Economic Assistance in Fragile States* (Washington, DC: US Institute of Peace, 2016), https://www.usip.org/sites/default/files/Fragility-Report-Policy-Brief-Applying-Compact-Model-of-Economic-Assistance-in-Fragile-States_0.pdf.

35. John Norris, *A Better Approach to Fragile States: The Long View* (Washington, DC: Center for American Progress, 2016), https://cdn.americanprogress.org/wp-content/uploads/2016/06/20123009/LongViewFragileStates-report.pdf.

[United States Government] departments or agencies to support an HN government and security forces, or an international organization. However, where there is no alternative competent lead organization or as national objectives dictate, the military force must be prepared to plan and execute USG stabilization efforts until it becomes feasible to transition that responsibility to another organization noted above.[36]

Civilian-military communication benefits from increased cross-agency assignments of personnel. These include service by USAID Foreign Service officers as development advisers and by State Department Foreign Service officers as political advisers to U.S. unified combatant commands and the assignment of military personnel to the Department of State and to USAID's Office of Civilian-Military Cooperation.

The Department of Defense also operates a Peacekeeping and Stability Operations Unit at the U.S. Army War College, with the mission of promoting "the collaborative development and integration of Peace and Stability capabilities across the U.S. government and the international community. The unit provides training for military and civilian personnel, disseminates publications, and facilitates information exchange."[37]

As indicated in the above-quoted passage from the Joint Chiefs' stabilization doctrine, the Department of Defense preference is for civilian leadership in civilian actions. But the department's ultimate position is that the military will be prepared to act if civilian counterparts are not able to assume leadership. Department of Defense Instruction 3000.05 states:

> The Department of Defense shall be prepared to lead stability operations activities to establish civil security and civil control, restore essential services, repair and protect critical infrastructure, and deliver humanitarian assistance until such time as it is feasible to transition lead responsibility to other U.S. government agencies, foreign governments and security forces, or international governmental organizations.[38]

The evolution of the U.S. Africa Command illustrates the emerging division of responsibilities among U.S. government agencies in a region where a number of countries with fragile situations are confronting multiple challenges of security, governance, and development.[39] The appropriate

---

36. Joint Chiefs of Staff, *Stability*, Joint Publication 3-07 (Washington, DC: Department of Defense, 2016), http://www.dtic.mil/doctrine/new_pubs/jp3_07.pdf, x. See also Joint Chiefs of Staff, *Counterinsurgency. Joint Publication 3-24.* (Washington, DC: Department of Defense, 2013), http://www.dtic.mil/doctrine/new_pubs/jp3_24.pdf.

37. Peacekeeping and Stability Operations Unit website, http://pksoi.armywarcollege.edu.

38. Department of Defense Instruction 3000.05, September 16, 2009, section 4(a)(3), http://dtic.mil/whs/directives/corres/pdf/300005p.pdf.

39. See National Defense University, "Interview with Ambassador Princeton N. Lyman and Ambassador Johnnie Carson," *PRISM* 6, no. 4 (2017): 3–13, http://cco.ndu.edu/Portals/96/Documents/prism/prism_6-4/1-Carson.pdf?ver=2017-05-12-110302-463. See also David E. Brown, *AFRICOM at Five Years: The Maturation of a New U.S. Combatant Command* (Carlisle: U.S. Army War College Press, 2013), https://ssi.armywarcollege.edu/pdffiles/PUB1164.pdf; Oluwaseun Tella, "AFRICOM: Hard or Soft Power Initiative?," *African Security Review* 25, no. 4 (2016): 393–406.

balance of civilian and military instruments to respond to those challenges remains a subject of debate.[40]

THE EU APPROACH

The European Union adopted an approach to situations of fragility in 2007. The European Commission's analysis called for comprehensive and coordinated engagement through whole-of-government approaches. It recognized the need in each case for "a differentiated, articulated and holistic response, articulating diplomatic action, humanitarian aid, development cooperation and security."[41]

In 2013 the European Commission and the High Representative for Foreign Affairs and Security Policy issued a joint communication on such a comprehensive EU approach to external conflicts and crises. The communication set out eight measures to enhance EU coherence and effectiveness in conflict or crisis situations: (1) develop a shared analysis of the situation or challenge, (2) define a common strategic vision, (3) focus on prevention, (4) mobilize the different strengths and capacities of the European Union, (5) commit to the long term, (6) link internal and external policies and action, (7) make better use of the role of EU delegations, and (8) work in partnership with other international and regional actors.

This approach reflected appreciation of both the development and the security dimension of responding to fragility. It emphasized that the overall objectives were sustainable peace and development, which required that the European Union have a long-term vision for its short-term engagements and actions. In this regard, it acknowledges that "sustainable development and poverty eradication require peace and security, and the reverse is equally true. . . . The connection between security and development is therefore a key underlying principle in the application of an EU comprehensive approach."[42]

40. See the various views expressed by participants at a September 2017 U.S. Institute of Peace Conference, "U.S. Signals Africa Policy Shifts," https://www.usip.org/publications/2017/09/us-signals-africa-policy-shifts. See also the analysis of underlying causes of extremist violence in Africa in UNDP, *Journey to Extremism in Africa: Drivers, Incentives and the Tipping Point for Recruitment* (New York: UNDP, 2017), http://journey-to-extremism.undp.org/content/downloads/UNDP-JourneyToExtremisim-report-2017-english.pdf.

41. European Commission, *Towards an EU Response to Situations of Fragility: Engaging in Difficult Environments for Sustainable Development, Stability and Peace* (Brussels: Publications Office of the EU, 2007), http://eur-lex.europa.eu/LexUriServ/LexUriServ.do?uri=COM:2007:0643:FIN:EN:PDF. See also Council of the European Union, *Council Conclusions on a EU Response to Situations of Fragility* (Brussels: Publications Office of the EU, 2007), http://www.consilium.europa.eu/uedocs/cms_Data/docs/pressdata/en/gena/97177.pdf; and *European Parliament Resolution of 15 November 2007 on the EU Response to Situations of Fragility in Developing Countries* (Brussels: Publications Office of the EU, 2007), http://www.europarl.europa.eu/sides/getDoc.do?pubRef=-//EP//TEXT+TA+P6-TA-2007-0540+0+DOC+XML+V0//EN.

42. European Commission and High Representative of the European Union for Foreign Affairs and Security Policy, *The EU's Comprehensive Approach to External Conflict and Crises* (Brussels: Publications Office of the EU, 2013), http://www.eeas.europa.eu/archives/docs/statements/docs/2013/131211_03_en.pdf. See also Council of the European Union, *Council Conclusions on the EU's Comprehensive Approach* (Brussels: Publications Office of the EU, 2014), https://www.consilium.europa.eu/uedocs/cms_Data/docs/pressdata/EN/foraff/142552.pdf.

At the invitation of the council, the commission and high representative developed action plans to carry forward the EU comprehensive approach in 2015 and in 2016–2017. Both action plans address the following topics: (i) joint analysis, options, and strategic vision; (ii) conflict prevention; (iii) making better use of EU delegations; (iv) linking policies and internal and external action; and (v) work in partnerships.[43]

The comprehensive approach has been the subject of extensive commentary, which has centered on the difficulties of implementation. In particular, observers have emphasized that the differences in organizational mandates, responsibilities, perspectives, cultures, expertise, staffing practices, and resources discussed above are impediments not only in Brussels but also in each of the member states and in the relations between Brussels and EU members. An additional layer of complexity, it has been noted, is that each fragile situation requires its own strategy from prevention to preparedness, response, and management.[44]

A number of published comments on gaps between the European Union and its member states include descriptions of the policies of EU countries (e.g., the United Kingdom, Germany, France, Sweden, Denmark, and the Netherlands). A noteworthy observation is the evident admiration for the progress made by the United Kingdom with an approach that "is highly strategic, structured and targeted," with system-wide national concepts linking the major institutional actors and providing them "with pooled financial and human resources to perform comprehensively."[45]

---

43. European Commission and High Representative of the European Union for Foreign Affairs and Security Policy, *Taking Forward the EU's Comprehensive Approach to External Conflict and Crises—Action Plan 2015* (Brussels: Publications Office of the EU, 2015), http://data.consilium.europa.eu/doc/document/ST-7913-2015-INIT/en/pdf; European Commission and High Representative of the European Union for Foreign Affairs and Security Policy, *Comprehensive Approach to External Conflicts and Crises—Action Plan 2016–17* (Brussels: Publications Office of the EU, 2016), http://data.consilium.europa.eu/doc/document/ST-11408-2016-INIT/en/pdf.

44. See, for example, Volker Hauck and Camilla Rocca, *Gaps between Comprehensive Approaches of the EU and EU Member States* (Maastricht: European Centre for Development Policy Management, 2014); Fernanda Faria, *What EU Comprehensive Approach? Challenges for the EU Action Plan and Beyond* (Maastricht: European Centre for Development Policy Management, 2014), http://ecdpm.org/wp-content/uploads/BN71-What-EU-Comprehensive-Approach -October-2014.pdf; Mark Furness, *Let's Get Comprehensive: European Union Engagement in Fragile and Conflict- Affected Countries* (Bonn: German Development Institute, 2014), https://www.die-gdi.de/uploads/media/DP_5.2014 .pdf; Clare Castillejo, *Fragile States: An Urgent Challenge for EU Foreign Policy* (Madrid: Fundación para las Relaciones Internacionales y el Diálogo, 2015), http://fride.org/download/WP126_Fragile_states.pdf.

45. Volker and Rocca, *Gaps between Comprehensive Approaches of the EU and EU Member States*, 35. For a discussion of EU members (UK, Germany, and the Netherlands), see also Weiss, Spanger, and Meurs, *Diplomacy, Development and Defense*. For the UK, the Netherlands, Sweden, and the United States, see Andreas Wittkowsky and Ulrich Wittkampf, *Pioneering the Comprehensive Approach: How Germany's Partners Do It* (Berlin: Center for International Peace Operations, 2013), http://www.zif-berlin.org/fileadmin/uploads/analyse/dokumente/veroeffentlichungen /ZIF_Policy_Briefing_Andreas_Wittkowsky_Ulrich_Wittkampf_Jan_2013.pdf; Ministry of Foreign Affairs, Ministry of Defence, Ministry of Justice, *Denmark's Integrated Stabilization Engagement in Fragile and Conflict-Affected Areas of the World* (Copenhagen: Danish International Development Agency, 2013), http://danida-publikationer.dk/upload /microsites/um/ebooks/stabiliseringspolitik_uk_web.pdf; Federal Ministry for Economic Cooperation and Development, *Development-Oriented Transformation in Conditions of Fragile Statehood and Poor Government Performance* (Germany) (Bonn: Federal Ministry for Economic Cooperation and Development, 2007), https://www.bmz.de/en /publications/archiv/type_of_publication/strategies/konzept153.pdf; Anette Hoffmann, *Policy Review: International*

Within the United Kingdom, DFID policies have included participation with the Foreign and Commonwealth Office and the Ministry of Defense in a Building Stability Overseas Strategy and a 2015 aid strategy that emphasizes investments to tackle the causes of instability, insecurity, and conflict; tackle crime and corruption; and strengthen resilience and responses to crises. Partly in response to SDG 16, the strategy commits to allocate 50 percent of DFID's annual budget to fragile states and regions.[46] A 2017 report by the National Audit Office indicates that implementation of the aid strategy has encountered some challenges of interagency coordination and coherence.[47]

The European Union continues efforts to improve the acceptance and effectiveness of its comprehensive approach. The 2016 Global Strategy for the EU foreign and security policy identified an integrated approach to conflicts and crises as a priority. The strategy pledged a multidimensional, multiphased approach to prevention, resolution, and stabilization while avoiding premature disengagement.

The strategy also included commitments to preemptive peacebuilding efforts and the development of "a political culture of acting sooner in response to the risk of violent conflict." A concluding paragraph on this topic describes the EU approach to fostering space for a political economy of peace. This approach calls for greater synergies between humanitarian and development assistance, trade, and restrictive measures (such as sanctions) combined with diplomacy.[48]

In June 2017, the commission and the high representative followed up on the comprehensive approach with a communication on a strategic approach to resilience in the European Union's external action. This communication called attention to the need to address more effectively the challenge of "structural fragility" in protracted crises, especially in situations "where poverty, population growth, climate change, rapid urbanization, competition for limited resources, conflict and violent extremism are creating whole regions of instability."[49] Also in 2017, the European Union

and Dutch Policies in the Field of Socio-Economic Development in Fragile Settings (Netherlands), Occasional Paper No. 10 (Wageningen, Netherlands: IS Academy on Human Security in Fragile States, 2014), https://www.clingendael.nl/sites/default/files/International%20and%20Dutch%20policies%20in%20the%20field%20of%20socio-economic%20development%20in%20fragile%20settings%20-%20Hoffmann.pdf.

46. United Kingdom, National Security Strategy and Strategic Defence and Security Review 2015, November 2015, https://www.eda.europa.eu/docs/default-source/procurement/uk-national-security-strategy-and-strategic-defence-security-review-2015.pdf. See HM Treasury and DFID, UK Aid: Tackling Global Challenges in the National Interest (London: Chancellor of the Exchequer, 2015), https://www.gov.uk/government/uploads/system/uploads/attachment_data/file/478834/ODA_strategy_final_web_0905.pdf.

47. National Audit Office, Managing the Official Development Assistance Target—A Report on Progress (London: National Audit Office, 2017), https://www.nao.org.uk/wp-content/uploads/2017/07/Managing-the-Official-development-Assistance-target-a-report-on-progress-Summary.pdf.

48. European Union, Shared Vision, Common Action: A Stronger Europe—A Global Strategy for the European Union's Foreign and Security Policy (Brussels, 2016), http://www.eeas.europa.eu/archives/docs/top_stories/pdf/eugs_review_web.pdf.

49. European Commission and High Representative of the European Union for Foreign Affairs and Security Policy, Joint Communication to the European Parliament and the Council: A Strategic Approach to Resilience in the EU's External Action (Brussels: Publications Office of the EU, 2017b), https://eeas.europa.eu/sites/eeas/files/join_2017_21_f1_communication_from_commission_to_inst_en_v7_p1_916039.pdf. See also the one-year report on the EU Global Strategy, European Commission and High Representative of the European Union for Foreign Affairs and Security Policy, From Shared Vision to Common Action: Implementing the EU Global Strategy Year 1 (Brussels: Publications Office of the EU, 2017a), http://europa.eu/globalstrategy/sites/globalstrategy/files/full_brochure_year_1.pdf.

established a new European Fund for Sustainable Development, which calls for attention to the financing needs of countries experiencing fragility.[50]

THE NEW DEAL FOR ENGAGEMENT IN FRAGILE STATES APPROACH

On the eve of the 2011 Busan Partnership conference, the g7+ group of conflict-affected states and their international partners in the IDPS developed the New Deal for Engagement in Fragile States.[51] The New Deal set forth proposed peacebuilding and statebuilding goals, an implementation approach that relies on country leadership and ownership, and a set of commitments to build trust and use resources effectively. This framework was welcomed at Busan and has attracted broad international support.[52]

The New Deal clearly reflects a perspective from the development side of the security-development continuum. Nevertheless, its foundational set of five Peacebuilding and Statebuilding Goals (PSGs) is closely aligned with the desired end states set out in the more security-oriented Strategic Framework for Stabilization and Reconstruction developed by the U.S. Institute for Peace and the U.S. Army Peacekeeping and Stability Operations Institute. This alignment, as illustrated in Table 3.1, demonstrates the consistency of the stability and development objectives in efforts to overcome fragility and achieve societal resilience.

Pursuit of the New Deal goals is guided by the "FOCUS" methodology. (FOCUS stands for Fragility assessment; One vision, one plan; Compact; Use peacekeeping and statebuilding goals to monitor; Support political dialogue and leadership.) The process begins with a country-led assessment of the causes of fragility and sources of resilience. That assessment informs the preparation of a national vision and plan, developed in consultation with civil society. In turn, the plan is implemented through a compact to ensure consideration of stakeholder views, donor harmonization and coordination, and coherent programming. Performance of implementation is monitored by reference to the peacebuilding and statebuilding

---

50. European Parliament and Council, *Regulation Establishing the European Fund for Sustainable Development (EFSD), the EFSD Guarantee and the EFSD Guarantee Fund* (Brussels: Publications Office of the EU, 2017), http://data.consilium .europa.eu/doc/document/PE-43-2017-INIT/en/pdf.

51. See Andries Odendaal, *The Road to the New Deal: Working Papers, 2010–2011 International Dialogue Working Groups*, IDPS (2012), https://www.pbsbdialogue.org/media/filer_public/3f/ef/3fef42cb-88cb-43d3-ad3b-c248b1bb 261a/the_road_to_the_new_deal.pdf. The 20 members of the g7+, 35 members of the INCAF, and 40 members of the Civil Society Platform for Peacebuilding and Statebuilding constitute the International Dialogue. They are listed at International Dialogue, "Participating Countries and Organisations," https://www.pbsbdialogue.org/en/id/participating -countries-and-organisations.

52. Busan Conference, *Busan Partnership for Effective Development Cooperation*, 8, para. 26. The compact approach had earlier been adopted by the United States for the MCC (discussed above). Also see Ashraf Ghani and Clare Lockhart, *Fixing Fragile States: A Framework for Rebuilding a Fractured World* (New York: Oxford University Press, 2008), chapter 7 (169–197), which advocated in 2008 a strategy of "double compacts" by country leadership with the international community and the country's citizens, very consistent with the New Deal approach.

Table 3.1. Goals and End States

New Deal Peacebuilding/Statebuilding Goals	USIP–U.S. Army Strategic Framework End States
Legitimate Politics—Foster inclusive political settlements and conflict resolution.	Stable Government—Ability of the people to share, access, or compete for power through nonviolent political processes and to enjoy the collective benefits and services of the state.
Security—Establish and strengthen people's security.	Safe and Secure Environment—Ability of the people to conduct their daily lives without fear of systematic or large-scale violence.
Justice—Address injustices and increase people's access to justice.	Rule of Law—Ability of the people to have equal access to just laws and a trusted system of justice that holds all persons accountable, protects their human rights, and ensures their safety and security.
Economic Foundations—Generate employment and improve livelihoods.	Sustainable Economy—Ability of the people to pursue opportunities for livelihood within a system of economic governance.
Revenues and Services—Manage revenue and build capacity for accountable and fair service delivery.	Social Well-Being—Ability of the people to be free from want of basic needs and to coexist peacefully in communities with opportunities for advancement. [See also Stable Government, above.]

Sources: IDPS, *A New Deal for Engagement in Fragile States*; U.S. Institute of Peace and U.S. Army Peacekeeping and Stability Operations Institute, *Guiding Principles for Stabilization and Reconstruction*, 2–9.

goals and supported by inclusive dialogue together with assistance for capacity building and participation.

Trust-building commitments to support aid provision, effective management, and alignment of resources are the subject of the TRUST values. These are transparency, risk-sharing, use and strengthening of country systems, strengthening capacities, and timely and predictable aid.

The g7+ has developed a Fragility Spectrum tool to help countries conduct sound self-assessments. This tool provides an analytical framework with a menu of possible indicators for each of the five peacebuilding and statebuilding goals at each of five stages of progress from crisis to rebuild and reform, transition, transformation, and resilience.[53] The Fragility Spectrum is supported by an IDPS Guidance Note on Fragility Assessments, which explains the purposes of an assessment and provides guidance on timing and methodology.[54]

---

53. g7+, *Note on the Fragility Spectrum*.

54. IDPS, *Guidance Note on Fragility Assessments: Seventh International Dialogue Working Group Meeting on New Deal Implementation* (Abidjan: IDPS, May 2014a), http://www.pbsbdialogue.org/media/filer_public/96/fb/96fb5ae4 -7b0d-4007-bf9e-1ed869db21da/rd_4_fragility_assessment_guidance_note_final.pdf.

New Deal implementation efforts have been initiated in 12 countries.[55] However, progress has been limited. A number of assessments have been conducted, several compacts have been finalized, and New Deal goals have been included in national plans. However, the implementation process is complex and demanding, especially for countries with weak institutions, limited capabilities, and skeptical publics. Equivocal leadership commitments have been major impediments in several cases. Also, maintaining collaboration for an extended period among all the national and international participants is challenging in divided political and social environments.[56]

An IDPS monitoring report in 2014 made extensive recommendations for possible improvements based on the initial three years of experience. A subsequent independent review summarized these recommendations as falling into five areas:

- Orient political dialogue, country plans, implementation modalities, monitoring, and mutual accountability toward the peacebuilding and statebuilding goals;

- Agree on a smaller set of measurable priorities within compacts to deliver visible results and build confidence and greater tolerance for risk;

- Build whole-of-government ownership within g7+ and OECD members for implementing the New Deal, by extending the principles across ministries in the g7+ and beyond bilateral aid agencies in the OECD;

- Make headway on using country systems by taking an incremental approach to increasing the use of instruments that build country systems over time; and

- Orient New Deal implementation away from global dialogue to country-level implementation.[57]

The New Deal has been criticized on various grounds: being too technical and not sufficiently political, being inflexible and cumbersome, being too much influenced by aid donors and not enough by local stakeholders, and failing to convert its principles into actual practice. At the same time, it has been acknowledged, as suggested in the above-cited independent review,

> Harnessing opportunities and managing risks will require national ownership of efforts to address fragility and its causes. Retreat from the New Deal principles, and the challenges now highlighted by it, should be inconceivable.

55. Specific countries and summaries of actions taken in each of them are published at IDPS, "New Deal Implementation—Country Level Progress," http://www.pbsbdialogue.org/en/new-deal/implementation-progress.

56. See Jacob Hughes, Ted Hooley, Siafa Hage, and George Ingram, *Implementing the New Deal for Fragile States* (Washington, DC: Brookings Institution, 2014), https://www.brookings.edu/wp-content/uploads/2014/07/global_20160811_new_deal_fragile_states.pdf. See also Laurence Chandy, Brijna Seidel, and Christine Zhang, *Aid Effectiveness in Fragile States: How Bad Is It and How Can It Improve?* (Washington, DC: Brookings Institution, 2016), https://www.brookings.edu/wp-content/uploads/2016/12/global_121616_brookeshearer.pdf.

57. IDPS, *New Deal Monitoring Report 2014* (n.p.: IDPS, 2014b), http://www.pbsbdialogue.org/media/filer_public/a5/df/a5dfd621-00a5-4836-8e20-8fff3afd1187/final_2014_new_deal_monitoring_report.pdf; Hearn, *Independent Review of the New Deal for Engagement in Fragile States.* The predominant role of g7+ finance ministers and the need for broadened support among government ministries is discussed in Rocha de Siqueira, *Managing State Fragility*, 172–177.

However, significant efforts will be needed to increase the New Deal's traction and relevance in the SDGs era.[58]

The various reviews of New Deal implementation are consistent in recognizing the need for greater emphasis on the political dimension of transformation. Among other things, they highlight needs for diplomatic dialogue to accompany donor assistance; expanded awareness of and support for the New Deal beyond the narrow group of officials and civil society activists who are already familiar with it; simplified, less burdensome, and better-prioritized agendas consistent with the capabilities of local ownership and existing political, economic, and social constraints; and more consistent and sustained international support that respects local ownership and supports growing local capabilities.

Ultimately, though, successful implementation in each situation will depend upon whether a sufficient cross-section of national and international stakeholders can be convinced that the New Deal approach has a reasonable prospect for advancing shared values and interests, and that the potential results are worth the risks they involve and the sustained efforts they demand. In other words, there must be achieved a combination of sufficient and sustained commitment to the goals together with capabilities to implement national plans and evidence of progress to sustain political and popular support.

Members of the IDPS met in Stockholm in April 2016 and pledged to renew their commitment "to bring together countries seeking to move beyond fragility and conflict, their development partners, and civil society representatives committed to supporting their efforts." Their pledge included agreement to

- strengthen the International Dialogue's commitment to peacebuilding, statebuilding, and conflict prevention by addressing the root causes of violence, conflict, and fragility, and by improving our systems to ensure inclusion and accountability and to rebuild trust between state and citizens;

- use the New Deal principles to achieve the SDGs in fragile and conflict-affected situations;

- provide smarter, more effective, and more targeted development support in fragile and conflict-affected situations, especially in protracted humanitarian crises and in g7+ countries; and

- strengthen and expand partnerships to improve responses to conflict by forging broader, deeper, and more effective coalitions for peacebuilding and statebuilding.[59]

THE UN APPROACH

Peacebuilding and statebuilding are central to the purposes of the United Nations. The first UN peacekeeping mission and the first UN mediator were deployed in 1948. Since then, peace operations have become a growing part of the global agenda. While precise figures are subject to

---

58. Hearn, *Independent Review of the New Deal for Engagement in Fragile States*, 60–61.

59. IDPS, "Stockholm Declaration on Addressing Fragility and Building Peace in a Changed World," April 5, 2016, 2, http://www.government.se/contentassets/8c2491b60d494dd8a2c1046b9336ee52/stockholm-declaration-on-addressing-fragility-and-building-peace-in-a-changing-world.pdf.

change, more than 100,000 individuals are now serving "under the blue flag" in many places around the world.

UN peace operations have certainly had success in moderating dangerous tensions, containing conflict, and supporting postconflict reconstruction. At the same time, there has been dissatisfaction with the ability of the concerned UN entities to implement their respective mandates in a coherent and coordinated way in a changing global environment. That dissatisfaction appears to be due, in part, to discord within the UN system, including tension between the desire for operational effectiveness and concern not to legitimize intervention in sovereign member states.

In the 1992 Agenda for Peace, Secretary-General Boutros Boutros-Ghali introduced the notion of peacebuilding, with an emphasis on avoiding relapse into conflict.[60] This was followed in 2000 by the report of the Panel on United Nations Peace Operations (Brahimi report), which made sensible recommendations about matching mission objectives with conditions on the ground, matching mandates with resource availabilities, and improving communication with the Security Council.[61]

The present century has seen a continuing procession of reviews and reforms in the UN system. These include the following:

In 2004, the High-Level Panel on Threats, Challenges and Change recommended strengthening of peacebuilding capability, noting that there was "no place in the United Nations system explicitly designed to avoid State collapse and the slide to war or to assist countries in their transition from war to peace."[62] To fill this gap, the panel recommended the creation of a Peacebuilding Commission.

In 2005, with the urging of Secretary-General Kofi Anan's far-reaching report *In Larger Freedom: Towards Development, Security and Human Rights for All*,[63] the World Summit adopted the elements of the UN Peacebuilding Architecture (PBA): the Peacebuilding Commission (PBC), the Peacebuilding Support Office (PBSO), and the Peacebuilding Fund (PBF). The focus of the mandate was "to bring together all relevant actors to marshal resources and to advise on and propose integrated strategies for post-conflict peacebuilding and recovery" rather than conflict prevention.[64]

---

60. UN, *An Agenda for Peace*. See UNGA Res. 47/120.

61. UN, *Report of the Panel on United Nations Peace Operations*.

62. UN, *A More Secure World: Our Shared Responsibility*, Report of the Secretary-General's High-Level Panel on Threats, Challenges and Change (New York: UN, 2004), chap. 15, 83, http://www.un.org/en/peacebuilding/pdf/historical/hlp_more_secure_world.pdf.

63. UN, *In Larger Freedom: Towards Development, Security and Human Rights for All*, UN Doc. A/59/2005 (New York: UN, 2005a), para. 114, https://documents-dds-ny.un.org/doc/UNDOC/GEN/N05/270/78/PDF/N0527078.pdf?Open Element.

64. UN, *2005 World Summit Outcome*, UNGA Res. 60/1 (New York: UN, 2005b), paras. 97–105, http://www.un.org/womenwatch/ods/A-RES-60-1-E.pdf. See also UN, *The Peacebuilding Commission*, UNGA Res. 60/180 (New York: UN, 2005c), http://www.un.org/ga/search/view_doc.asp?symbol=A/RES/60/180, which operationalized the PBC mandate. Structural issues in the design of the PBA have been a challenge from the outset. For example, creating the PBC as an advisory body, reporting to both the Security Council and the General Assembly, necessarily limited its authority.

In 2010, supported by the secretary-general's report on peacebuilding in the immediate aftermath of conflict,[65] the United Nations undertook a review of the peacebuilding architecture (PBA). The review made recommendations intended to increase relevance, flexibility, performance, support, ambition, and understanding of the PBA. The review also identified as key issues the complexity of peacebuilding, the imperative of national ownership, the illusion of sequencing, the urgency of resource mobilization, the importance of the contribution of women, and the need for connection with the field.[66]

The 2015 High-Level Independent Panel on Peace Operations (HIPPO) and the Advisory Group of Experts on Peace Operations (AGE) prepared separate reports for a 10th anniversary review of UN peacebuilding work. The incisive AGE report urged replacement of fragmented UN "silos" with a unity of the peace and security, human rights, and development pillars of the United Nations. This would enable a flourishing of a concept of sustaining peace "along the arc leading from conflict prevention . . . through peacemaking and peacekeeping, and on to post-conflict recovery and reconstruction."[67]

The HIPPO report called for four essential shifts:

- Politics must drive the design and implementation of peace operations.
- The full spectrum of UN peace operations must be used more flexibly to respond to changing needs on the ground.
- A stronger, more inclusive peace and security partnership is needed for the future.
- The UN Secretariat must become more field focused and UN peace operations must be more people centered.

Consistent with the AGE report, the HIPPO recommended prioritizing conflict prevention, unifying UN strengths, and working in partnership with others.[68] The secretary-general submitted a report on implementation in September 2015,[69] and in April 2016 the General Assembly adopted a resolution of support.[70]

---

65. UN, *Report of the Secretary-General on Peacebuilding in the Immediate Aftermath of Conflict*, UN Doc. A/63/881–S/2009/304 (New York: UN, 2009), http://www.un.org/en/peacebuilding/pbso/pdf/s2009304.pdf.

66. UN, *Review of the United Nations Peacebuilding Architecture*, UN Doc. A/64/868–S/2010/393 (New York: UN, 2010), http://www.un.org/ga/search/view_doc.asp?symbol=A/64/868.

67. UN, *Challenge of Sustaining Peace: Report of the Advisory Group of Experts on the Review of the Peacebuilding Architecture*, UN Doc. A/69/968—S/2015/490 (New York: UN, 2015b), http://www.un.org/ga/search/view_doc.asp?symbol=A/69/968.

68. UN, *Report of the High-Level Independent Panel on Peace Operations on Uniting Our Strengths for Peace: Politics, Partnership and People*, UN Doc. A/70/95—S/2015/446 (New York: UN, 2015a), http://www.un.org/en/ga/search/view_doc.asp?symbol=S/2015/446.

69. UN, *The Future of United Nations Peace Operations: Implementation of the Recommendations of the High-Level Independent Panel on Peace Operations*, Report of the Secretary-General, UN Doc. A/70/357—S/2015/682 (New York: UN, 2015c), http://www.un.org/en/ga/search/view_doc.asp?symbol=S/2015/682.

70. UN, *Review of the United Nations Peacebuilding Architecture*.

A 2015 Global Study on implementing Security Council Resolution 1325 marked the 15th anniversary of the council's call for increased participation of women in policy decisionmaking and implementing operations relating to conflict prevention, management, and resolution and peace processes.[71] This thoughtful and comprehensive global study (more than 400 pages in length) benefited from broad participation. It addressed many issues and offered many recommendations for future action. In particular, it called for application of a gender lens to all issues that come before the Security Council, an earmark of 15 percent for programs impacting women in all peace and security funding, and efforts toward stronger gender architecture at the United Nations.[72]

The three 2015 studies contained many common observations and recommendations, reflecting the changing drivers of instability, different kinds of conflict, and evolving thinking about the importance of key issues such as prevention and respect for local ownership, capability, and commitment. The common themes across the three principal reports (AGE, HIPPO, and Global Study) were summarized as follows in a 2016 report by the Norwegian Institute of International Affairs:

- The nature of conflict is changing, with increased violent extremism and changed implications for civilians, including women and girls.

- There is increasing importance for the women, peace, and security agenda in the United Nations' work, with need for greater gender sensitivity and inclusion.

- Prevention must be prioritized with a focus on sustaining peace and maintaining a long-term focus.

- Local ownership needs to look beyond governments to include broad consultative engagement, shifting toward people-centered, inclusive processes.

- Peacebuilding must be understood as an inherently political process.

---

71. UN, *Security Council Resolution 1325, October 31, 2000, on Women, Peace and Security* (New York: UN, 2000b), https://documents-dds-ny.un.org/doc/UNDOC/GEN/N00/720/18/PDF/N0072018.pdf?OpenElement.

72. Radhika Coomaraswamy, *Preventing Conflict, Transforming Justice, Securing the Peace* (New York: UN Women, 2015), 394–397, http://wps.unwomen.org/pdf/en/GlobalStudy_EN_Web.pdf. The study's general guidelines and recommendations were summarized as follows: No to militarization, yes to prevention; women, peace, and security must be respected as a human rights mandate; mediators of peace processes and leadership of UN field missions must be proactive with regard to women's participation; the presence of women makes peace sustainable; perpetrators must be punished and justice must be transformative; localization of peacebuilding programs must involve the participation of women at every level and be supplemented by a comprehensive security plan to protect women and girls in the aftermath of conflict; funding women peacebuilders and respecting their agency is one important way of countering extremism; all key actors must play their role toward a well-informed Security Council that applies a gender lens to all issues that come before it; across the board; 15 percent of all funding for peace and security is to be earmarked for programs impacting women; the UN must work toward a strong gender architecture. See also UN Security Council Res. 2242 of October 13, 2015, *Women, Peace, and Security* (2015e), http://www.securitycouncilreport.org/atf/cf/%7B65BFCF9B-6D27-4E9C-8CD3-CF6E4FF96FF9%7D/s_res_2242.pdf, which endorsed the Global Study; and the secretary-general's report to the Security Council of September 29, 2016, *Report of the Secretary-General on Women and Peace and Security*, UN Doc. S/2016/822 (2016a), http://www.un.org/en/ga/search/view_doc.asp?symbol=S/2016/822, which reports on further implementation of Security Council Res. 1325.

- The United Nations needs to pay more attention to local context and dynamics, adopting a field focus and context awareness while avoiding one-size-fits-all template approaches.

- Militarized solutions are an obstacle to lasting peace and the United Nations' tendency to privilege military responses to violent conflict is counterproductive.

- It is important to partner with others, including regional organizations, economic actors, and grass-roots networks.

- There is a need for greater leadership, professionalization, and accountability within the United Nations.

- There should be greater integration and coherence within the UN system, with commitment and participation from the Security Council and coordination between the human rights, development, and security pillars.[73]

While these reports urge an integrated approach to peacebuilding, they all approach the subject with a security orientation. It is encouraging to see in them some of the same thinking about the endogenous nature of societal transformation that has influenced development cooperation. Prominent references to inclusive local ownership and respect for local systems, context-appropriate adaptation to the local political and economic environment, and sustainability with a long-term focus are all consistent with the mainstream of thought about effective development cooperation.

Also encouraging is the movement toward expanding partnerships that can foster more coherent responses to multidimensional fragility challenges. For example, in April 2017 the United Nations and World Bank announced the establishment of a new framework by which the two organizations will seek to build resilience and sustain peace in conflict areas. According to their joint statement, the United Nations and World Bank will collaborate to do the following:

- Identify and reduce critical multidimensional risks of crisis, and prevent violent conflict in relevant countries or regions within the mandate of both institutions;

- Coordinate support for situations of protracted crisis, including aligning strategies, objectives, and collective outcomes, in particular for populations affected by forced displacement, and based on joint analyses and assessments;

- Develop joint analyses and tools to help enable more effective solutions; and

- Scale up impact, by leveraging existing financing and comparative advantages, and ensuring that operational policies, frameworks, and tools used by both organizations facilitate cooperation and improve efficiency and complementarity.[74]

73. Eli Stamnes and Kari M. Osland, *Synthesis Report: Reviewing UN Peace Operations, the UN Peacebuilding Architecture and the Implementation of UNSCR 1325* (Oslo: Norwegian Institute of International Affairs, 2016), 20–24, http://www.un.org/pga/70/wp-content/uploads/sites/10/2016/01/NUPI_Report_2_16_Stamnes_Osland.pdf.

74. UN–World Bank Joint Statement on Signing of New Framework to Build Resilience and Sustain Peace in Conflict Areas, April 22, 2017, http://www.worldbank.org/en/news/press-release/2017/04/22/un-world-bank-joint-statement -on-signing-of-new-framework-to-build-resilience-and-sustain-peace-in-conflict-areas. The new framework builds

The UN–World Bank collaboration has produced an important study with an emphasis on prevention: *Pathways for Peace: Inclusive Approaches to Preventing Violent Conflict*.[75]

From the development side of the United Nations, UNDP has long advocated for a broad notion of human security that emphasizes human development.[76] It has collaborated with the World Bank for more than a decade to support statebuilding in fragile environments.[77] Following the adoption of the New Deal, UNDP established a New Deal Implementation Support Facility, with four key deliverables: country support, support for travel to international meetings of the g7+ and the IDPS, stronger capacity for the g7+ secretariat, and (added in 2015) support for implementation of the SDGs.[78]

As a related matter, UNDP is tracking support for implementation of SDG 16 (promote peaceful and inclusive societies for sustainable development, provide access to justice for all, and build effective, accountable, and inclusive institutions at all levels).[79] (The *Sustainable Development Goals Report 2017* indicates only limited and uneven progress toward SDG 16.)[80] Understandably, UNDP has given primary emphasis in its strategic plan to integrated support for democratic governance, conflict prevention, and peacebuilding. It seeks to apply this integrated approach across all settings, recognizing that fragility, conflict, and violence can affect any country or society.[81]

The UN peacebuilding system has been the subject of highly critical analysis, especially in the context of postconflict environments.[82] One demonstration of the system's inconsistency concerns attitudes regarding the New Deal. As noted above, UNDP has had a program of support for the g7+ and for the IDPS since the New Deal was established. However, some Peacebuilding

---

on a history of previous UN–World Bank collaboration. See IDA, *Special Theme: Fragility, Conflict and Violence* (Washington, DC: IDA, 2016), 10, http://documents.worldbank.org/curated/en/652991468196733026/pdf/106182-BR -IDA18-Fragility-Conflict-and-Violence-PUBLIC-IDA-R2016-0140.pdf.

75. Main messages from this study were published in November 2017. See World Bank and UN, *Pathways for Peace: Inclusive Approaches to Preventing Violent Conflict—Main Messages and Emerging Policy Directions* (Washington, DC: World Bank, 2017), https://openknowledge.worldbank.org/bitstream/handle/10986/28337/211162mm.pdf?sequence =2&isAllowed=y. Publication of the final, book-length report is expected early in 2018.

76. See UNDP, *Human Development Report 2005*, 168–177.

77. See Sue Ingram, *State-Building: Key Concepts and Operational Implications in Two Fragile States—The Case of Sierra Leone and Liberia* (New York: UNDP and World Bank, 2011), http://www.undp.org/content/undp/en/home /librarypage/crisis-prevention-and-recovery/statebuilding_conceptsandoperationalimplicationsintwofragilestat.html.

78. See UNDP, *New Deal Implementation Support Facility: 2015 Annual Report* (New York: UNDP, 2016a), http://www .undp.org/content/undp/en/home/librarypage/democratic-governance/undp-new-deal-facility-annual-report-2015 .html.

79. *UNDP Support to the Implementation of Sustainable Development Goal 16*.

80. UN, *Sustainable Development Goals Report 2017*, 49–53.

81. See Muggah, Sisk, Piza-Lopez, Salmon, and Keuleers, *Governance for Peace*; UNDP, *Building Inclusive Societies and Sustaining Peace through Democratic Governance and Conflict Prevention: An Integrated Approach* (New York: UN, 2016d), http://www.undp.org/content/undp/en/home/librarypage/democratic-governance/building-inclusive -societies-and-sustaining-peace-through-democr.html.

82. See, for example, Álvaro de Soto and Graciana del Castillo, "Obstacles to Peacebuilding Revisited," *Global Governance* 22, no. 2 (2016): 209–227, which concludes that "the twenty-five year record of UN peacebuilding is indeed bleak."

Commission members reportedly have regarded the New Deal as "a Western-dominated agenda that subordinated development to security concerns." This negative view, according to one report, places the PBC at risk of "being marginalized from much of the action in the field."[83]

Deliberations over UN peace operations continue. An April 2016 General Assembly resolution announced the assembly's decision to convene at its 72nd session a high-level meeting on efforts undertaken and opportunities to strengthen the United Nations' work on sustaining peace. The resolution also invited the secretary-general to report at least 60 days prior to that high-level meeting on a broad range of issues relating to peacebuilding and sustaining peace. Secretary General Antonio Guterres is expected to submit his report early in 2018 and the high-level meeting is scheduled for April 2018.[84]

In his initial address to the Security Council on January 10, 2017, Secretary-General Guterres made very clear his views on the importance of an integrated international approach to the interrelated issues of security and development, with an emphasis on prevention:

> The interconnected nature of today's crises requires the international community to connect global efforts for peace and security, sustainable development and human rights, not just in words, but in practice. The 2030 Agenda for Sustainable Development and the General Assembly and Security Council resolutions on sustaining peace demonstrate strong intergovernmental support for an integrated approach. The challenge now is to make corresponding changes to our culture, strategy, structures and operations.

On that occasion, the secretary-general observed that it had "proven very difficult to persuade decisionmakers at both the national and international levels to make prevention their priority." He announced that he had appointed a Special Adviser on Policy, whose main task would be "to map the prevention capacities of the UN system and to bring them together into an integrated platform for early detection and action." The objective, he said, was to link the reform of the peace and security architecture with the reform of the UN development system.[85]

---

83. Hearn, *Independent Review of the New Deal for Engagement in Fragile States*, 7. See Jenna Slotin and Molly Elgin-Cossart, *Why Would Peace Be Controversial at the United Nations? Negotiations toward a Post-2015 Development Framework* (New York: New York University Center on International Cooperation, 2013), http://cic.nyu.edu/sites/default/files/negotiations_post_2015_dev_framework.pdf. See also "Playing UN Politics" in Rocha de Siqueira, *Managing State Fragility*, 190–193.

84. UN, *Review of the United Nations Peacebuilding Architecture*, UNGA/RES/70/262 (New York: UN, 2016c). See also UNSC S/RES/2282 (New York: UN, 2016), http://www.securitycouncilreport.org/atf/cf/%7B65BFCF9B-6D27-4E9C-8CD3-CF6E4FF96FF9%7D/s_res_2282.pdf; UN, "Session on Peacebuilding and Sustaining Peace," April 20, 2017, http://www.un.org/pga/71/2017/04/20/ession-on-peacebuilding-and-sustaining-peace; UN, "Acceptance Remarks by President-Elect for the 72nd Session of UNGA," May 31, 2017, http://www.un.org/pga/71/2017/05/31/acceptance-remarks-by-president-elect-for-the-72nd-session-of-unga/.

85. UN, "Secretary-General, in First Address to Security Council since Taking Office, Sets Restoring Trust, Preventing Crises as United Nations Priorities," UN Meetings Coverage, January 10, 2017, https://www.un.org/press/en/2017/sc12673.doc.htm.

THE OECD APPROACH

The OECD has played a major role as a thought leader in the evolution of research, analysis, and practice in the international response to the multidimensional challenges of fragility. Initially separate work streams on improving aid effectiveness in difficult environments[86] and on dealing with issues of peace and conflict[87] have merged into a more coherent focus on fragility.

The OECD Principles for Good International Engagement in Fragile States and Situations, adopted in 2007, set out a long-term vision in 10 propositions accompanied by brief explanatory paragraphs. They call on international actors to do the following:

1. Take context as the starting point.

2. Do no harm.

3. Focus on statebuilding as the central objective.

4. Prioritize prevention.

5. Recognize the links between political, security, and development objectives.

6. Promote nondiscrimination as a basis for inclusive and stable societies.

7. Align with local priorities in different ways in different contexts.

8. Agree on practical coordination mechanisms between international actors.

9. Act fast . . . but stay engaged long enough to give success a chance.

10. Avoid pockets of exclusion.[88]

In 2008 the OECD/DAC combined its former Fragile States Group and its Conflict, Peace, and Development Network into the INCAF. An important early INCAF product was an in-depth study of international support for statebuilding. This study included an extensive literature review and, drawing on six diverse case studies, analyzed how donor activities might have positive or negative impacts on local political processes.[89] With INCAF leadership, the OECD has produced dozens of additional guidance documents, including a collaborative survey in 2010 on monitoring the application of the

---

86. See OECD, "Working for Development in Difficult Partnerships."

87. See OECD, "Conflict, Peace and Development Cooperation on the Threshold of the 21st Century" (Paris: OECD, 1997/2001).

88. See OECD, *Principles for Good International Engagement in Fragile States & Situations* (Paris: OECD, 2007), http://www.oecd.org/dac/conflict-fragility-resilience/docs/38368714.pdf. The principles were originally developed to complement the partnership commitments set out in the Paris Declaration on Aid Effectiveness. (Paragraphs 37–39 of the declaration address the issue of aid effectiveness in fragile states.) The OECD Principles emphasize the relevance of violent conflict and the interdependence of political, security, economic, and social challenges.

89. OECD, *Do No Harm: International Support for Statebuilding* (Paris: OECD, 2010a), https://www.oecd.org/dac/conflict-fragility-resilience/docs/do%20no%20harm.pdf.

OECD Principles[90] and a 2016 policy paper that consolidates lessons learned in three thematic areas: building institutional fitness, aspiring to deliver change, and leaving no one behind.[91]

INCAF members have been active participants in the IDPS. Through this mechanism, developed and developing countries, international organizations, and civil society groups collaborate in a spirit of partnership, including on the implementation of the New Deal for Engagement in Fragile States, described above.[92]

The OECD annual reports on fragility, now titled "States of Fragility," explore five dimensions of fragility (economic, environmental, political, security, and societal), provide analysis on topical issues, and assess factors contributing to fragility in situations of concern in accordance with the recently adopted multidimensional OECD fragility framework, described in Chapter 2. The framework is intended to serve as a tool for advocacy on fragility issues, monitoring and reporting on high-risk contexts, and guiding policy responses and risk management.[93]

THE APPROACHES OF OTHER INTERNATIONAL DEVELOPMENT INSTITUTIONS

International development institutions have played growing roles within their areas of responsibility to support recovery and development in fragile and conflict-affected environments. Increasingly, those roles have expanded from a focus on postconflict reconstruction to include increased emphasis on conflict prevention and on an expanding range of topical areas related to overcoming fragility and enhancing resilience.

Often, these institutions have endeavored to coordinate their efforts. Many of them came together in 2007 on a set of common goals, guiding principles, and operational approaches to improve and harmonize their collaboration in fragile situations.[94] The goals were to strengthen national ownership of recovery and reform, build capacity and accountability in national institutions, and contribute to

90. OECD, *Monitoring the Principles for Good International Engagement in Fragile States and Situations: Global Report* (Paris: OECD, 2010b), http://www.keepeek.com/Digital-Asset-Management/oecd/development/monitoring-the-principles -for-good-international-engagement-in-fragile-states-and-situations_9789264090057-en#.WSii04WcHIU#page1. (The global report was based on a number of country reports.)

91. OECD, *Good Development Support in Fragile, At-Risk and Crisis-Affected Contexts* (Paris: OECD, 2016a), http://www .oecd-ilibrary.org/docserver/download/5jm0v3s71fs5-en.pdf?expires=1495834258&id=id&accname=guest&checksum=5 32D556653116777C3CD938624F0801B. Numerous additional publications are available on the OECD website page for conflict, fragility, and resilience: http://www.oecd.org/dac/conflict-fragility-resilience/cfr-publications.htm.

92. IDPS participants are listed at https://www.pbsbdialogue.org/en/id/participating-countries-and-organisations.

93. The 2016 report focused on understanding violence; the 2015 report addressed meeting post-2015 ambitions. The OECD fragility framework is presented in chapter 3 of OECD, *States of Fragility, 2016*, 69–84.

94. Participants in this harmonized approach included the AfDB, ADB, European Bank for Reconstruction and Development, Inter-American Development Bank, Islamic Development Bank, and World Bank. See MDB Working Group, *Toward a More Harmonized Approach to MDB Engagement in Fragile Situations* (Washington, DC: World Bank, 2007), http://siteresources.worldbank.org/INTLICUS/Resources/Report_of_the_MDB_Working_Group.pdf. The agreement is summarized in IMF, *The Fund's Engagement in Fragile States and Post-Conflict Countries: A Review of Experience— Issues and Options* (Washington, DC: IMF, 2008), 54, https://www.imf.org/external/np/pp/eng/2008/030308.pdf.

peacebuilding through economic and social programs. In addition to this harmonized approach, each of the institutions has its own policies and practices. Several of these are described below.

World Bank

The World Bank was initially cautious in its response to demands that it assume an expanded role in the growing number of conflicts in the 1990s. The Bank's 1997 framework for engagement in postconflict reconstruction expressed a number of reservations. These included statements affirming that the Bank is not a world government with an unlimited mandate, that it is not in charge of peacemaking or peacekeeping, that it does not question the political character of a member and does not interfere in a member's domestic political affairs, that it does not operate in the territory of a member without its approval, and that it is not a relief agency.

With these cautions in mind, the framework called for attention to opportunities to help prevent conflict in at-risk situations and, where conflict has occurred, recommended a five-stage phased approach—from maintaining a watching brief to preparing a transitional support strategy, transitioning to early reconstruction activities, undertaking postconflict reconstruction, and ultimately returning to normal lending operations.[95] To help operationalize this framework the Bank established a Post-Conflict Unit, later renamed the Conflict Prevention and Reconstruction Unit, and now called the Fragility, Conflict and Violence Group.

A parallel development was the Bank's response to poorly performing recipients of assistance. The Task Force on Work of the World Bank Group in Low Income Countries under Stress (LICUS) was formed in 2001 and led by distinguished development practitioners Ngozi Okonjo-Iweala and Paul Collier. Its mission was to examine how the development community "can best help chronically weak-performing countries get onto a path leading to sustained growth, development, and poverty reduction." This was an aid effectiveness agenda. The September 2002 report of the LICUS Task Force recommended an approach "to facilitate policy and institutional change while improving basic social outcomes by focusing on a few reforms that are feasible in sociopolitical terms, around which capacity building and outcome monitoring can be coordinated." The task force summarized this approach in a series of 22 propositions, which addressed many issues.[96]

Among other things, the propositions called for prioritizing opportunities for large and quick payoffs in the most seriously deficient areas (macro, structural, or social), with emphasis on improving governance and policies favorable for private economic activity. Other recommendations included a focus on knowledge transfer, a preference for grants rather than loans, a stress on accountability, early attention to security service reform, restoration of domestic order, and financial capacity building. The report also reiterated the limited role of the World Bank, which "does not have a mandate to be a political actor."[97]

In seeking to operationalize the 1997 framework and the 2002 task force recommendations, the World Bank's Conflict Prevention and Reconstruction Unit produced a number of guidance documents. In 2003 the Bank collaborated with the United Nations and the government of Germany to

95. World Bank, *Post-Conflict Reconstruction: The Role of the World Bank*.

96. World Bank, *World Bank Group Work in Low-Income Countries under Stress*.

97. Ibid.

prepare a practical guide on multilateral needs assessments in conflict situations. The guide specified that each assessment should reflect the political processes underpinning the postconflict transition, reflect in-depth understanding of national realities, and ensure that the assessment results are owned by national (transitional) authorities.[98]

A major evaluation of the LICUS initiative in 2006 found that the Bank had improved its operational readiness to deal with volatile LICUS conditions, had developed guidance on a number of issues, improved access to financing, and contributed to improved donor coordination at the international policy level. On the other hand, the review pointed out that the Bank's country strategies did not sufficiently internalize political understanding, that donor coordination remained inadequate at the country level, and that the Bank's new focus on statebuilding had not been accompanied by evidence of how past weaknesses would be avoided and how improved capacity and governance would be achieved.

In particular, the evaluators called for increased donor focus on political analysis in strategy design, rather than treating issues such as political patronage and corruption as technical in nature. Recommendations included the following:

- Clarification of the scope and content of the Bank's statebuilding agenda and strengthening design and delivery of capacity development and governance support.

- Development of aid-allocation criteria to ensure that LICUS are neither under- or over-aided.

- Strengthening internal support for LICUS work within the Bank and removing duplication and fragmentation.

- Reassessing the value added by the LICUS approach after three years with the benefit of additional experience.[99]

In the following year (2007) the World Bank adopted a new policy on operational approaches and financing in fragile states. This policy recognized that a number of countries faced issues similar to those on the World Bank's technical list of fragile states, including higher-income states. The policy used the term "fragile situations" as a generality and limited the use of "fragile states" to those on the Bank list.[100]

A 2010 research report by the GSDRC, a partnership of research institutes, think tanks, and consultancy organizations, found a number of recurring negative findings in current literature about World Bank performance in fragile states. The GSDRC findings included the following:

---

98. World Bank, *Practical Guide to Multilateral Needs Assessments in Post-Conflict Situations* (Washington, DC: World Bank, 2004), http://documents.worldbank.org/curated/en/224281468762594718/pdf/298220PAPER0SDP0WP151Web .pdf (also published as a UN document). Other World Bank guidance documents are listed in an appendix to the guide.

99. Soniya Carvalho, *Engaging with Fragile States: An IEG Review of World Bank Support to Low-Income Countries under Stress* (Washington, DC: World Bank, 2006), http://documents.worldbank.org/curated/en/418191468142504861 /pdf/382850Revised01gile0states01PUBLIC1.pdf.

100. World Bank, *Operational Approaches and Financing in Fragile States.*

- The Bank's approach to statebuilding and economic reform in fragile states remains overly technical and pays insufficient attention to informal institutions, power relations, and social dynamics.

- The integration of conflict concerns in its programs and policies remains uneven across the organization and limited in depth.

- The Bank's results framework still measures success largely in technical terms and may act as a disincentive for staff to take risks that could have positive long-term impacts.[101]

The *WDR* 2011 on conflict, security, and development had a major influence on thinking about fragility. It moved beyond the development effectiveness agenda that had dominated the World Bank's traditional approach to fragile situations, asserting at the outset that insecurity "has become a primary development issue of our time" and that the report's central message was "that strengthening legitimate institutions and governance to provide citizen security, justice, and jobs is crucial to break cycles of violence." That is clearly a political message.

The *WDR* focused on the dynamics of preventing cycles of violence and the roles of the World Bank and others in the international community in linking diplomacy, development, security, and humanitarian support. It recommended a four-track global response for security and development:

- Integrated, specialized assistance for citizen security, justice, and jobs;

- Reform of internal agency systems to provide rapid action to restore confidence and promote long-term institution building;

- Act regionally and globally to reduce external stresses; and

- Marshal support from lower-, middle-, and higher-income countries and from global and regional institutions to reflect the changed landscape of international policy and assistance.[102]

Following this landmark report, the World Bank undertook to operationalize it with a six-point commitment:

- Work to make country assistance strategies for fragile and conflict-affected situations more focused on fragility.

- Strengthen partnerships on development, security, and justice.

- Increase attention to jobs and private-sector development.

- Realign results and risk management for fragile and conflict-affected situations.

- Reduce financing volatility.

- Strive for global excellence in the World Bank's work in fragile and conflict-affected situations.[103]

---

101. GSDRC, *The World Bank in Fragile States* (Birmingham: GSDRC, 2010), http://www.gsdrc.org/docs/open/hd651.pdf.

102. World Bank, *World Development Report 2011*.

103. World Bank, *Operationalizing the 2011 World Development Report: Conflict, Security, and Development* (Washington, DC: World Bank, 2011b), http://siteresources.worldbank.org/DEVCOMMINT/Documentation/22884392/DC2011-0003(E)

The World Bank demonstrated an enduring commitment to improve its own performance with respect to fragility issues by undertaking two more evaluations: one in 2013 on low-income countries and a second, on middle-income countries, in 2016.

The 2013 evaluation of World Bank assistance to low-income countries reviewed initial efforts to operationalize the 2011 *WDR*. It found substantial progress in improving country strategies and seeking to reduce financial volatility. It also reported some progress in efforts to achieve global excellence through improved knowledge and communication. On the other hand, it found little progress in strengthening Bank programs on development, security, and justice or in increasing attention to jobs and private-sector development.

Significant recommendations included the following:

- Develop a more suitable mechanism to define fragile and conflict-affected situations or states (FCS), at least to integrate indicators of conflict, violence, and political risks;

- Respond to the environment in postconflict countries, including with respect to violence and constraints on economic empowerment in gender programs;

- Develop a realistic medium- to long-term framework for inclusive growth and jobs, ensuring synergies and collaboration across the three Bank Group institutions; and

- Adapt the International Finance Corporation (IFC) and the Multilateral Investment Guarantee Agency's (MIGA) business models, risk tolerance, product mix, sources of funds, staff incentives, procedures, and processes to be more responsive to the special needs of FCS.[104]

The 2016 evaluation of World Bank experience in middle-income countries was limited in two significant ways.

First, the countries selected for review were neither IDA eligible nor the locations of international peacekeeping or peacebuilding missions. Thus, they were not fragile and conflict-affected countries according to the World Bank definition. Therefore, they were not covered by the policy and programming standards that the Bank applies to "fragile states." (See the discussion of the World Bank definition in Chapter 2.)

Second, the evaluation's selection criteria included only countries with histories of prolonged conflict and violence as well as significant World Bank programs. This caused the evaluation to focus on a somewhat narrow group of countries, using somewhat different policy standards than those applicable to the low-income countries studied in the 2013 evaluation.[105]

WDR2011.pdf; World Bank, *Fragility and Conflict: Changing the Paradigm* (Washington, DC: World Bank, 2014a), http://siteresources.worldbank.org/EXTLICUS/Resources/sixpoints-brochure.pdf. Evidence of a more expansive approach in World Bank analysis regarding fragility is found in a 2013 study that focused on social cohesion—levels of trust and collaboration—as a crucial element of reducing fragility. See Marc et al., *Societal Dynamics of Fragility.*

104. World Bank, *World Bank Group Assistance to Low-Income Fragile and Conflicted-Affected States.*

105. The other selection criteria were differing levels of income and institutional capacity and locations different geographic regions. The selected countries were Colombia, Honduras, Indonesia, Jordan, Lebanon, Nigeria, Pakistan, Philippines, Sri Lanka, and Uganda.

The 2016 evaluation noted the importance of continuous presence and rapport with local actors, especially for addressing longer-term development challenges. In this regard, the evaluators thought institutional and staff incentives for engagement in conflict situations were lagging behind the World Bank's stated strategic approach. They also noted the limitations of the World Bank's definition of fragile and conflict-affected states, which excludes most middle-income countries.

Also, the evaluators found that fragility-conflict-violence-specific diagnostic work by the World Bank was not common in the middle-income countries, perhaps because it was not formally required other than for the few such countries on its Harmonized List of Fragile Situations. In addition, they found only limited focus on gender issues in conflict-affected areas in middle-income countries. They also recommended the development of institutional incentives and thematic guidance to foster more systematic collaboration with the United Nations and other partners.[106]

Together, these evaluations should contribute to the continued evolution and refinement of World Bank policy and practice in responding to the complex challenges of fragility. In particular, addressing the artificial distinction between low-income "fragile and conflict-affected states" and middle-income "fragility, conflict, and violence situations" would provide greater consistency and coherence. Also, the adaptation to more political and context-sensitive approaches at the country level appears to need continuing attention.

Looking ahead, the World Bank made fragility, conflict, and violence a special theme for the 18th replenishment of IDA, to be carried out in 2017–2020, noting that these factors constituted "one of the most pressing challenges for achieving the SDGs" and affected "countries beyond the list of [FCS] and can have regional and/or global dimensions."[107] In addition, the 2017 "Forward Look" by the Development Committee anticipates IFC partnerships with middle-income countries and enhanced advisory engagement to promote investment in fragile situations.[108]

International Monetary Fund

The IMF expanded its emergency assistance in natural disasters in 1995 to also include postconflict assistance. However, it did not establish a specific policy for fragile situations at that time. The IMF increased the flexibility of access to emergency assistance in 2000 and created new concessional financing framework for low-income countries, the Poverty Reduction and Growth Trust (PRGT), in 2010.[109]

---

106. World Bank, *World Bank Group Engagement in Situations of Fragility, Conflict, and Violence: An Independent Evaluation* (Washington, DC: World Bank, 2016), https://openknowledge.worldbank.org/bitstream/handle/10986/24915 /World0Bank0Gro0dependent0evaluation.pdf?sequence=4&isAllowed=y.

107. IDA, *Toward 2030*, 41–44. See also IDA, *Special Theme*. The theme of "fragility, conflict and violence" replaced a special theme in IDA 17 titled "fragile and conflict-affected states," reflecting some evolution in World Bank thinking about fragility.

108. World Bank and IMF Development Committee, *Forward Look—A Vision for the World Bank Group in 2030: Progress and Challenges* (Washington, DC: World Bank, 2017b), 4 and 7, paras. 15 and 23, http://siteresources.worldbank .org/DEVCOMMINT/Documentation/23745169/DC2017-0002.pdf.

109. See IMF, *The Fund's Engagement in Fragile States and Post-Conflict Countries* (Washington, DC: IMF, 2008) https://www.imf.org/external/np/pp/eng/2008/030308.pdf. See also IMF, *Fact Sheet: Financing the IMF's Concessional*

A 2008 review took note of international efforts to devise a broad and coordinated approach to fragility as well as the role of the several areas of IMF support: macroeconomic policy advice, surveillance to track performance, technical assistance for capacity building, and financial assistance.

The review identified four major issues based on experience:

- Fragile states are often unable to mobilize timely international support;

- They have limited access to debt relief;

- They need time to overcome institutional and political weaknesses, build capacity, and use resources effectively; and

- The IMF needs to coordinate with others.

The review concluded that the IMF needed to use a more graduated, long-term approach with opportunity for more informed, step-by-step efforts to assess macroeconomic prospects and management capacity. Toward that end, the staff recommended a new, medium-term approach specifically for low-income, fragile countries. Directors saw merit in the finding that a more graduated, long-term approach was appropriate, but they did not approve the review's recommendation for a specific new facility for fragile states.[110]

A further internal review in 2011 revisited the issues of fragility in considerable depth, including consideration of the World Bank's 2011 *WDR* and other ongoing international activities. The review's summary conclusion was as follows:

> In a nutshell, effective support means engaging at an early stage and being prepared to stay engaged over the long haul, embracing a philosophy of carefully sequenced reforms tailored to improvements in capacity, helping country authorities deliver "quick wins" to the population, and, in this process, building the legitimacy of the state.

Proposed changes in IMF engagement included the following:

- Use of the Rapid Credit Facility (RCF) for low-income countries and a Reformed Nonconcessional Emergency Facility for middle-income countries;

- Greater flexibility and realism in policy design, with an emphasis on job creation, inclusive growth, planning for contingencies, and a streamlined policy agenda focused on key areas of statebuilding; and

- Deeper understanding by IMF staff of the risks and political nuances associated with the specific fragile situation, supported by incentives for staff to accept assignments that involve living and working in the difficult circumstances.[111]

Lending to Low-Income Countries (Washington, DC: IMF, 2016b), http://www.imf.org/external/np/exr/facts/pdf/concess lending.pdf.

110. IMF, *The Fund's Engagement in Fragile States and Post-Conflict Countries.*

111. IMF, *Macroeconomic and Operational Challenges in Countries in Fragile Situations* (Washington, DC: IMF, 2011), https://www.imf.org/external/np/pp/eng/2011/061511a.pdf. Note the language change from "fragile states" to

This analysis was discussed in the IMF Executive Board, resulting in the issuance in 2012 of new operational guidance for IMF staff. The guidance note specified seven principles for engagement with low- and middle-income countries in fragile situations:

- More explicit consideration of the political context, understanding of sociopolitical constraints, and opportunities and risks with respect to social cohesion;

- A well-tailored pace of macroeconomic adjustment, bearing in mind institutional capacity constraints;

- A focus on sequencing of reforms, with a view to opportunities for quick wins to build public support;

- Explicit attention to inclusive growth, job creation, and social safety nets;

- Tailoring structural reforms to priority sectors and socially critical issues so as not to overwhelm limited capacity and institutional weakness.

- Integrated capacity building to support effective implementation of key structural or institutional measures; and

- Contingency planning to ensure adequate room for maneuver in potentially volatile or unstable conditions.[112]

In 2015, staff examined the IMF's experience in implementing the above-described 2011 analysis and 2012 guidance. The examination included a number of case studies and an extensive survey of mission directors in the field. It concluded that a number of additional steps could be taken to strengthen the IMF's engagement with fragile states, with a focus on capacity building, access to financing, program design, and policy advice and support.[113]

In addition, the IMF's Independent Evaluation Office launched an evaluation in 2016 on the IMF and fragile states. The Evaluation Office invited public comment on a draft issues paper and then issued the final issues paper in July 2017.[114] In addition, a 2016 policy paper included an examination of the use of the RCF for fragile states.[115]

"countries in fragile situations." This reflects the trend to regard fragility as a temporary condition that can be overcome rather than the character of a country.

112. IMF, *Staff Guidance Note on the Fund's Engagement with Countries in Fragile Situations* (Washington, DC: IMF, 2012), http://www.imf.org/external/np/pp/eng/2012/042512.pdf.

113. IMF, *IMF Engagement with Countries in Post-Conflict and Fragile Situations—A Stocktaking* (Washington, DC: IMF, 2015), https://www.imf.org/external/np/pp/eng/2015/050715.pdf. This staff paper confirmed that the IMF continues to follow World Bank criteria for defining fragile states.

114. IMF, *The IMF and Fragile States: Issues Paper for an Evaluation by the Independent Evaluation Office* (Washington, DC: IMF, 2017b), http://www.ieo-imf.org/ieo/files/whatsnew/FS_Final%20Issues_Paper%207-25-17.pdf.

115. IMF, *Financing for Development: Enhancing the Financial Safety Net for Developing Countries—Further Considerations* (Washington, DC: IMF, 2016a), https://www.imf.org/en/Publications/Policy-Papers/Issues/2016/12/31/Financing-for-Development-Enhancing-the-Financial-Safety-Net-for-Developing-Countries-PP5076. See also IMF, *Fact Sheet: Financing the IMF's Concessional Lending to Low-Income Countries*.

The review and revision process continues with a 2017 policy paper on building fiscal capacity in fragile states. This paper distinguishes IMF technical assistance for fragile states from assistance for countries not designated as fragile. It also notes differences between fragile environments with immediate security challenges and those with more stable conditions. This policy was reviewed by the Executive Board in May 2017.[116]

African Development Bank

The AfDB adopted postconflict assistance policy guidelines in 2001 in recognition that the challenges faced in distinct postconflict situations required a concerted approach.[117] Continued study and accumulated experience led the AfDB to a strategy for enhanced engagement in fragile states in 2008. To implement that strategy, it created a Fragile States Unit and a Fragile States Facility to finance special needs relating to infrastructure, state capacity and accountability, arrears clearance, and technical assistance.[118]

An independent evaluation of the AfDB's assistance to fragile states in 2012 and a review by a high-level panel on fragile states in Africa[119] led to the development in 2014 of a new strategy on fragility in Africa with an emphasis on resilience. This strategy expressly acknowledges and seeks to reflect "the evolving international consensus on partnership modalities for addressing fragility as expressed in the New Deal for Engagement in Fragile States."[120]

The revised AfDB strategy is, indeed, in harmony with the New Deal approach. It is notable for its description of fragility as a transient condition resulting from "an imbalance between the strains and challenges faced by a society (internal or external or a combination thereof) and the society's ability to manage them." It recognizes that all countries "face issues of fragility which vary in their dimensions,

116. IMF, *Building Fiscal Capacity in Fragile States* (Washington, DC: IMF, 2017a), http://www.imf.org/en/Publications/Policy-Papers/Issues/2017/06/14/pp041817building-fiscal-capacity-in-fragile-state?cid=em-COM-123-35417.

117. AfDB, *Post-Conflict Assistance Policy Guidelines* (Abidjan: AfDB, 2001), https://www.afdb.org/fileadmin/uploads/afdb/Documents/Policy-Documents/32%20-EN%20-Bank_Group_Post-conflict_Assistance_Policy_Guidelines_-_Revised_%28Approval%29_01.pdf.

118. AfDB, *Strategy for Enhanced Engagement in Fragile* States (Tunis: AfDB, 2008), https://www.afdb.org/fileadmin/uploads/afdb/Documents/Policy-Documents/30736191-EN-STRATEGY-FOR-ENHANCED-ENGAGEMENT-IN-FRAGILES-STATES.PDF.

119. See AfDB, *Development Effectiveness Review 2012—Fragile States and Conflict-Affected Countries* (Tunis: AfDB, 2012), https://www.afdb.org/fileadmin/uploads/afdb/Documents/Project-and-Operations/Development_Effectiveness_Review_2012_-_Fragile_States_and_Conflict-Affected_Countries.pdf; AfDB, *Ending Conflict and Building Peace in Africa: A Call to Action* (Abidjan: AfDB, 2014b), https://www.afdb.org/fileadmin/uploads/afdb/Documents/Project-and-Operations/Ending_Conflict_and_Building_Peace_in_Africa-_A_Call_to_Action.pdf. See also Institute for State Effectiveness, *Institutional Reform of Development Organizations—Case Study: African Development Bank* (Washington, DC: Institute for State Effectiveness, 2009), http://stateeffective.wpengine.com/wp-content/uploads/2015/09/Institutional-Reform-of-Development-Organizations.pdf, which reviews the history of AfDB strategies and operations up to 2009.

120. AfDB, *African Development Bank Group Strategy for Addressing Fragility and Building Resilience in Africa* (Abidjan: AfDB, 2014a), 20, https://www.afdb.org/fileadmin/uploads/afdb/Documents/Policy-Documents/Addressing_Fragility_and_Building_Resilience_in_Africa-_The_AfDB_Group_Strategy_2014%E2%80%932019.pdf.

dynamics, and severity over time, as do countries' capacities to deal with them, i.e. their resilience." This approach causes the strategy to refer to "fragile situations" rather than "fragile countries."[121]

Asian Development Bank

The ADB had gained considerable experience with fragility before it adopted a formal policy in 2007 on "achieving development in weakly performing countries." This initial explicit approach drew upon the ADB's regional experience as well as its participation in the deliberative processes organized by the OECD and the World Bank, including the development of the harmonized approach to goals, guiding principles, and operational approaches agreed to by the multilateral development banks. The two "pillars" of this approach were identified as (i) selectivity and focus and (ii) strategic partnerships, which the ADB described as being consistent with the OECD's Fragile States Principles.

The 2007 ADB approach related to countries that had low performance scores or were considered to be in a conflict or postconflict situation. It also called attention to additional countries that exhibited some elements of weak performance. In each case, programs were designed with the principal purpose of improving country performance through instruments considered appropriate to the particular context. It emphasized capacity development to strengthen country ownership. The essence of the approach was moderation of the ADB's performance-based approach in selective cases to provide greater flexibility.[122]

Since then, the ADB has been active in reviewing and revising the specific elements of its approach to fragility, including in the selection of aid instruments, focus and direction of operations, application of business procedures, responses to the challenges of delivering effective aid, and field presence and supervision capacities.

In 2010 the ADB's Independent Evaluation Office undertook a study of the 2007 approach, which was generally favorable. It recommended greater flexibility in country classification, better planning for country-specific capacity development, greater flexibility in program design, and more consultation with partners on resource gaps.[123]

A 2010 management review of ADB experience since 2007 pointed to refinements that would support increased effectiveness. These included sustained field presence and long-term commitments

---

121. AfDB, *Operational Guidelines for the Implementation of the Strategy for Addressing Fragility and Building Resilience in Africa and for the Transition Support Facility* (Abidjan: AfDB, 2014c), 3, https://www.afdb.org/fileadmin /uploads/afdb/Documents/Policy-Documents/Operational_Guidelines_for_the_Implementation_of_the_Strategy _for_addressing_Fragility_and_building_Resilience_in_Africa_and_for_TSF_-APPROVED.pdf.

122. ADB, *Achieving Development in Weakly Performing Countries (The Asian Development Bank's Approach to Engaging with Weakly Performing Countries)* (Manila: ADB, 2007), https://www.adb.org/sites/default/files/institutional -document/32039/secm30-07.pdf.

123. ADB, *Special Evaluation Study: Asian Development Bank's Support to Fragile and Conflict-Affected Situations* (Manila: ADB, 2010a), https://www.oecd.org/derec/adb/47186709.pdf. See also ADB, *Management Response to the Special Evaluation Study* (Manila: ADB, 2010b), https://www.adb.org/sites/default/files/institutional-document/33219 /files/mr-ses-reg-2010-45.pdf.

in fragile situations, broader efforts in capacity development, intensification of strategic partnerships, and innovative ways to address aid volatility in the face of aid dependence in fragile situations.[124] In turn, the management review led to the publication of a staff handbook in 2012 and an operational plan in 2013.[125]

All these reviews and guidance documents drew on the ADB's own experience and also on international developments such as the establishment of the IDPS, the 2011 *WDR* on Conflict, Security and Development, the Busan Partnership Declaration, and the New Deal for Engagement in Fragile States.

An especially significant component of the ADB's work on fragile situations was the major project from 2012 to 2016 to enhance its engagement in fragile and conflict-affected situations. The enhancements included a distinctive fragility index, described in Chapter 2, as well as a sophisticated and differentiated approach to fragility assessment and capacity development.[126]

THE ROLE OF THE PRIVATE SECTOR

The international response to the economic dimension of fragility is centered on efforts to promote growth, entry into the formal economy, and job creation. The private-sector role is indisputably essential to those efforts. In addition, early inclusive economic progress that improves lives can facilitate the political and security dimensions of transitions to sustainable stability.

Private-sector development is a prominent feature of international development cooperation, including in fragile environments.[127] The international consensus is expressed in a number of widely endorsed instruments such as the Busan Partnership Declaration and the UN Sustainable Development Summit Declaration.[128]

The more fragile environments tend to be the most challenging places for doing business. There is a strong correlation among indicators of substantial fragility, slow growth, high

124. ADB, *ADB Engagement in Fragile and Conflict-Affected Situations, 2007–2009* (Manila: ADB, 2010c), https://www.adb.org/sites/default/files/page/59522/session-5-fragile-conflict-affected-situations.pdf.

125. ADB, *Working Differently in Fragile and Conflict-Affected Situations—The ADB Experience: A Staff Handbook* (Manila: ADB, 2012), https://www.adb.org/sites/default/files/institutional-document/33774/files/working-differently-conflict-affected-situations.pdf; ADB, *Operational Plan for Enhancing ADB's Effectiveness in Fragile and Conflict-Affected Situations* (Manila: ADB, 2013), https://www.adb.org/sites/default/files/institutional-document/33825/files/operational-plan-fcas.pdf.

126. See ADB, *Project Completion Report: Enhancing ADB's Engagement in Fragile and Conflict-Affected Situations* (Manila: ADB, 2016), https://www.adb.org/sites/default/files/project-document/189490/45328-001-tcr.pdf.

127. See, generally, José Di Bella, Alicia Grant, Shannon Kindornay, and Stephanie Tissot, *Mapping Private Sector Engagements in Development Cooperation* (Ottawa: North-South Institute, 2013), http://www.nsi-ins.ca/wp-content/uploads/2013/09/Mapping-PS-Engagment-in-Development-Cooperation-Final.pdf. With respect to fragile situations, see the literature review compiled in William Robert Avis, *Private Sector Engagement in Fragile and Conflict-Affected Settings* (Birmingham: GSDRC, 2016), http://www.gsdrcd.org/wp-content/uploads/2016/03/HDQ1331.pdf.

128. Busan Conference, *Busan Partnership for Effective Development Cooperation*, para. 32 (private sector and development); UN, *Transforming Our World*, 29, para. 67.

informality and unemployment, and low scores on the World Bank's Doing Business Index.[129] The effectiveness of private-sector development cooperation programs in fragile environments is often disappointing.[130] There is a substantial volume of literature on how results can be improved.[131]

While local businesses are the primary private-sector actors, international businesses have also engaged in constructive ways that contribute to peacebuilding and statebuilding. However, levels of foreign direct investment in fragile environments remain low. Surveys of international businesses have suggested that political risk, and inadequate access to political risk insurance, has been a limiting factor.

Historically, the rules and rate structures of risk mitigation authorities such as the World Bank's MIGA and the U.S. Overseas Private Investment Corporation (OPIC) have not been compatible with the most difficult environments. However, MIGA established a multicountry, donor-funded facility expressly for fragile and conflict-affected situations in 2013 and OPIC has invested substantial amounts in countries experiencing fragile situations. The regulation establishing the European Fund for Sustainable Development, adopted in 2017, authorizes preferential terms for guarantees in countries experiencing fragility. In addition, special country-specific arrangements have stimulated private investment in several fragile environments.[132]

---

129. The World Bank's economy rankings are based on costs and time involved in starting a business, dealing with construction permits, getting electricity, registering property, getting credit, protecting minority investors, paying taxes, trading across borders, enforcing contracts, and resolving insolvency. See the website at http://www.doingbusiness.org/rankings.

130. Chaoying Liu and Emily Harwit, in *The Effectiveness of Private Sector Development Interventions in Fragile and Conflict-Affected Situations*, examined evaluations from 23 countries and found that fewer than 50 percent had reached or exceeded intended impacts such as increased job creation or investment. Chaoying Liu and Emily Harwit, *The Effectiveness of Private Sector Development Interventions in Fragile and Conflict-Affected Situations: Evidence from Evaluations* (Washington, DC: International Finance Corporation, World Bank, 2016), https://openknowledge .worldbank.org/bitstream/handle/10986/28497/120073-WP-Systematic-review-of-PSD-interventions-in-FCS-PUBLIC .pdf?sequence=1&isAllowed=y. Simone Datzberger and Mike Denison, in *Private Sector Development in Fragile States*, offered very cautious observations on the benefits and potential risks associated with private-sector development programs in fragile and conflict-affected states (Simone Datzberger and Mike Denison, *Private Sector Development in Fragile States* [London: EPS Peaks, 2013], https://assets.publishing.service.gov.uk/media/57a08a2ced915d622c0005cf /Private_Sector_Development_in_Fragile_States.pdf).

131. See Mary Porter Peschka, *The Role of the Private Sector in Fragile and Conflict-Affected States* (Washington, DC: World Bank, 2011), http://documents.worldbank.org/curated/en/887641468163482532/pdf/620590WP0The0R0 BOX0361475B00PUBLIC0.pdf; Victor Odundo Owuor, *Firm Behavior in Fragile States* (Broomfield, CO: One Earth Future Foundation, 2017), http://oefresearch.org/sites/default/files/documents/publications/Firm_Behavior_Fragile _States.pdf.

132. See MIGA Brief on Conflict-Affected and Fragile Countries, https://www.miga.org/documents/conflict.pdf; OPIC, *Seven Approaches to Developing Projects in Fragile Governance Environments*; World Economic Forum, Global Agenda Council on Fragile States and Conflict Prevention, *The Role of the Private Sector in Fragile States: Catalyzing Investment for Security and Development* (Geneva: World Economic Forum, 2014), http://www3.weforum.org/docs /GAC14/WEF_GAC14_FragileStatesConflictPrevention_Report%20.pdf; European Parliament and Council, *Regulation establishing the European Fund for Sustainable Development (EFSD)*, articles 9(2)(d) and 10(2).

Efforts of the bilateral and multilateral development agencies to stimulate local private-sector development in fragile situations are complemented in important ways by international businesses. Collaborative arrangements such as public-private partnerships can help to mitigate risks that might otherwise inhibit private investment. A 2017 analysis from the Brookings Institution reports that "foreign investment is on the rise in fragile states" and that of 1,600 USAID public-private partnerships since 2001 "one-third are in . . . fragile states."[133]

The World Economic Forum's Global Agenda Council on Fragile States and Conflict Prevention undertook an extensive program of studies and surveys over several years. This effort included the examination of investments by businesses in situations with varying degrees of fragility. Case studies included, among others, Chevron's engagement with local communities in Nigeria; Mastercard's engagement, also in Nigeria, on financial inclusion of women; Nespresso and TechnoServe's support for rebuilding the coffee sector in South Sudan; and Roshan's investment in Afghanistan's telecommunications sector.

Six insights from the council's body of work were summarized in a 2016 report:

- A positive business case is essential; altruism alone is insufficient. A "triple win" scenario should generate financial returns for the companies and benefits to the local communities and governments.

- A functioning state with the right institutions needs to be in place to guarantee longer-term stability. Businesses should coordinate among multiple stakeholders and invest in regional frameworks for resilience and capacity building.

- Private business knowledge can support fragile governments and societies. However, this demands situational awareness, sensitivity to local context, and patience.

- Public-private collaboration can accelerate innovation and growth. This requires a high degree of flexibility and agility from all partners. And these undertakings are more likely to succeed when international donors can provide financial guarantees and political confidence in volatile settings.

- The local private sector is the engine of growth and must be actively included in any solution. In particular jobs are generated largely by small and medium enterprises.

- Business can contribute to transparent and effective management of revenues from exports of natural resources. This should be accompanied by investments in human, physical, and institutional capabilities to encourage diversified economies.

---

133. George Ingram and Jonathan Papoulidis, *Rethinking How to Reduce State Fragility* (Washington, DC: Brookings Institution, 2017), https://www.brookings.edu/blog/up-front/2017/03/29/rethinking-how-to-reduce-state-fragility. See also World Bank, *Promoting Foreign Investment in Fragile and Conflict-Affected Situations* (Washington, DC: World Bank, 2014c), https://openknowledge.worldbank.org/bitstream/handle/10986/20432/911900BRI0Box30D0VC0KNOW LEDGE0NOTES.pdf?sequence=1&isAllowed=y; OECD and World Economic Forum, *Blended Finance*, vol. 1: *A Primer for Development Finance and Philanthropic Funders* (Geneva: World Economic Forum, 2015), http://www3.weforum .org/docs/WEF_Blended_Finance_A_Primer_Development_Finance_Philanthropic_Funders.pdf.

The report concluded that businesses, public international institutions, and civil society organizations all have key roles to play in mitigating fragility and contributing to growth and productivity.[134]

Clearly, the private sector is a major stakeholder in the international response to fragility. In the current environment of growing reliance on an expanding variety of actors and an increased diversity of financing resources, the role of the private sector will be of increasing importance in efforts to achieve transitions from fragility to resilience.

CONCLUSIONS

This chapter has described in some detail the intensity of efforts by major international actors to adopt and refine optimum responses to fragility. It also conveys their repeated dissatisfaction and efforts to obtain better results. The pattern has been one of recurring policy reviews and evaluations, followed by refinements in policies and practices. This pattern bears out the judgment of the Fragility Study Group in 2016: "Across the U.S. government there is no clear or shared view of why, how and when to engage fragile states. These problems are not unique to the United States; no state or international body has fully cracked the fragility code."[135]

Because of this unsatisfactory situation, the study group recommended that the United States should, itself, work in a more integrated and coherent fashion; that it should better synchronize its efforts with international partners; and that it should improve its ability to help fragile states foster legitimate state-society relations. These recommendations echo the findings of the various reviews and evaluations by other international actors, as described above.

The record of recurring efforts to improve, disappointment with the results, reviews of experience, and adaptation of structures and operations has produced some broad trends. These include greater readiness to address the political as well as the technical aspects of fragility, deeper awareness of the importance of prevention, and recognition that societal transformation is a long-term process requiring a long-term commitment.

International efforts to date have also provoked incisive criticism of past practice, including expressions of concern about the failure of multiple international stakeholders to come together to address the interrelated dimensions of fragility in an integrated and coherent manner that is responsive to changing needs.[136]

---

134. World Economic Forum, *Responsible Private Sector Action to Address Fragility, Conflict and Violence* (Geneva: World Economic Forum, 2016a), http://www3.weforum.org/docs/WEF_Responsible_Private_Sector.pdf.

135. Burns, Flournoy, and Lindborg, *U.S. Leadership and the Challenge of State Fragility*, 8.

136. See Graciana del Castillo, *Obstacles to Peacebuilding* (New York: Routledge, 2017), in which the author analyzes the need for closer attention in ongoing interrelated political, security, social, and economic transitions to the evolving economic priorities as a country progresses from crisis to reconstruction and recovery to development.

Shaping Effective Strategies to Diminish Fragility and Promote Resilience

Fragile situations are contributing disproportionately to the world's violence, instability, poverty, and forced displacement. Erosion of the social contract and diminished resilience create risks to peace, stability, and sustainable development. They increase vulnerability to influence, and even domination, by destructive forces. And yet, a consistent approach for responding effectively to fragility has continued to elude the international community.

There are good reasons why this challenge has proven to be so difficult, and the reasons are interrelated.

First, fragility is a complex phenomenon. It has multiple and interrelated economic, environmental, political, security, and societal dimensions, each of which may vary in specific content and severity from time to time and from place to place. Particular situations may give rise to greater or lesser concern about any of these dimensions.

Second, an enormous variety of situations can give rise to fragility concerns. There are many reasons why a situation can overwhelm a society's capacity to cope. A given situation may involve some or all of the dimensions of fragility and may involve a region, a single country, or a community within a country. The geographic focus of concern may be large or small, rich or poor, historically unstable or afflicted by a recent shock, and may be experiencing conditions that are persistent or dynamic. Once deterioration occurs, fragility tends to be persistent. But some countries have made progress toward navigating transitions to restored resilience and renewed development. The World Bank noted in 2016 that "since the Bank started monitoring fragility in 2003, 20 countries have 'graduated' from [fragile and conflict-affected] status."[1]

---

1. IDA, *Special Theme*, 3. Removal from the World Bank list, however, does not necessarily mean that a country has overcome fragility challenges and become a resilient society. The countries identified as having "graduated" are Cambodia, Djibouti, Georgia, Lao PDR, Nepal, Sao Tome and Principe, Tajikistan, Uzbekistan, Vanuatu (better performing) and Angola, Cameroon, Republic of Congo, Equatorial Guinea, Malawi, Mauritania, Niger, Nigeria, and Papua New Guinea (less well performing). See the discussion of the variety of situations referred to as "failed states" in Call, "'Beyond the Failed State,'" 4.

Third, as discussed in Chapter 2, various international actors and analysts have chosen to define the multiple and interdependent dimensions of fragility in different ways and have selected different methodologies and indicators to measure their severity. Some approach fragility from a security perspective, while others view it as a development problem. These divergent perspectives bring together organizations that have very different responsibilities, experiences, time frames, expertise, staffing, and resources. Differing organizational cultures sometimes impede effective collaboration.

Fourth, international cooperation has become more complicated. The number, variety, and roles of international actors have multiplied. The expansion of actors has increased the range of perspectives, interests, and objectives that may be engaged. Global financing to address fragility has increased in volume and become much more diversified. The increased and more diversified financing has made additional demands on national and international management skills and expertise.

Participants now include traditional donors of development assistance, international peacebuilding organizations, emerging economies that participate in peacebuilding and in south-south and triangular cooperation, private-sector and civil society organizations, and old and new multilateral financing organizations. The expanded range of financing relies increasingly on public and private domestic resources and on commercial and private international flows. Official international flows have increased more slowly and have become a relatively minor part of total global financing.[2]

At the same time, countries experiencing fragility, especially small economies without substantial natural resource endowments, often have little capacity for domestic resource mobilization and little access to commercial flows. Official development finance programs provide some support to encourage private investment. However, their success in overcoming the reluctance of investors in difficult environments has been limited.[3] Many countries experiencing fragility, therefore, remain highly dependent on aid. For them, international assistance is essential to their efforts to achieve stability and pursue sustainable development.

LESSONS LEARNED

Despite these difficulties, extensive international experience, numerous case studies, and frequent evaluations and reviews of policies and practice have produced a substantial body of shared knowledge.

There has evolved a substantial consensus that the several dimensions of fragility manifest themselves along a continuum of severity that ranges from crisis to resilience. As one review suggests,

---

2. See AfDB, ADB, European Bank for Reconstruction and Development, European Investment Bank, Inter-American Development Bank, IMF, and World Bank, *From Billions to Trillions*.

3. See, for example, the lists of active projects of the United States at OPIC, "Active Optic Projects," https://www.opic.gov /opic-action/active-opic-projects; the World Bank's IFC, "World Bank Group Finances," https://finances.worldbank.org /Projects/IFC-Investment-Services-Projects/efin-cagm/data; and the European Investment Bank, "Projects Financed," http://www.eib.org/projects/loan/list/index?from=2015&region=6&sector=&to=2017&country.

"fragility has come to be understood less as a state typology, and more as a combination of conditions that together can prevent a political, economic and social system . . . from coping with external or internal stresses in a nonviolent manner."[4]

Individual situations are situated at different points along the continuum, with different trajectories toward one end of the spectrum or the other—toward resilience or toward crisis. Rather than identify some countries as "fragile" and treat them as different from states thought to be "not fragile," the increasingly preferred approach is to concentrate on the specific aspects of fragility that are the principal impediments to stability and development in each particular situation.

Persuasive research is demonstrating how an initial focus on a few key priorities is often preferable to a comprehensive reform agenda that might risk overcomplicating international cooperation, overtaxing the capabilities of some or all the parties concerned, and retarding the essentially endogenous process of building a stable and resilient society.

Some studies have recommended early attention to certain issues. Security sector reform, tax administration, anticorruption initiatives, growth and increased employment in the formal economy, and governance affecting private economic activity are examples of such recommended focus areas. These are all important and interrelated. However, the selection of priorities should be based on the circumstances of each situation as determined by inclusive processes. There is broad support for popular participation in establishing priorities, as contemplated by the New Deal. The value of proceeding in an inclusive manner seems particularly high in situations of weak legitimacy and high distrust between government authorities and citizens.

A sharply focused approach still requires thoughtful attention to the political, security, and development aspects of each situation. Whole-of-government approaches and coherent, integrated strategies, while remaining focused on key priorities, need to benefit from coordinated diplomatic, development, and military input, as relevant to the local context. Technocratic or simplistic approaches that do not account for the complex of context-specific political, economic, social, and security conditions will not suffice.

There is also a preference, in principle, for early warning to detect indications of deteriorating conditions and facilitate the timely initiation of preventive measures. The consensus on prioritizing prevention implies agreement that the world should not wait until a crisis erupts, after which risks would be greater, progress would be slower, costs would be higher, and prospects for success would be less favorable. However, there is still work to be done to learn the lesson that early warning has little value if it does not result in timely response. International actors are still more likely to respond to a crisis than to anticipate and prevent one.

Along with appreciation for the importance of early preventive action, there is broad recognition that transitions from fragility to resilience take a long time. This is a recurring theme in the various policy documents discussed in Chapter 3. As the OECD Principles succinctly put it, "act fast . . . but stay engaged long enough to give success a chance."[5] We have seen how early withdrawal of

---

4. Hoffmann, *Policy Review*, 13.

5. OECD, *Principles for Good International Engagement in Fragile States and Situations*, Principle 9. To the same effect, the IMF 2011 review concluded: "In a nutshell, effective support means engaging at an early stage and being prepared

international engagement risks the reversal of initial progress and the perpetuation of fragility. The shift in international attention away from Central America in the 1990s, despite a history of political conflict, the proliferation of arms, and severe poverty, inequality, and exclusion, illustrates the danger.[6] Renewed violence, insecurity, and migration have intensified in the present decade. Just as it may be tempting to delay needed preventive action, it may be tempting to withdraw before progress becomes sustainable.

Effective implementation remains problematic. In situations where immediate security issues are prominent, those issues are likely to be the dominant influence in policy decisions, to the detriment of political and development considerations. (This tendency has prompted some understandable criticism.)[7] And where security issues are not so pressing, there is a greater risk that development practitioners, diplomats, and security experts may engage independently rather than in a coherent, integrated effort. In any case, there is a risk of tension between the need for initial concentration on a limited number of key priorities and the desire by multiple actors to be engaged.

Among the lessons learned, one is key to sorting out competing priorities and responsibilities. That is the widespread recognition of the endogenous, experiential nature of statebuilding and development processes and the need for international cooperation to be adaptive and conducive to results that are "viable, legitimate and relevant—i.e., politically supportable and practically implementable."[8] This recognition is evident in the New Deal's approach to engagement "to support country-owned and -led pathways out of fragility" and in the policies of other international actors. The New Deal approach is closely related to the Busan Partnership principles of local ownership, focus on results, inclusive partnerships, and mutual accountability and transparency, as discussed in Chapter 3.

ACHIEVING MORE EFFECTIVE STRATEGIES

The Fragility Study Group, in its September 2016 report, recommended a future direction for U.S. policy. The report drew upon the substantial body of experience and analysis that informs our understanding of fragility—what the study group called "collective wisdom." Elements of this body

---

to stay engaged over the long haul." IMF, *Macroeconomic and Operational Challenges in Countries in Fragile Situations*, 30.

6. See the analysis in Caroline Moser and Ailsa Winton, *Violence in the Central American Region: Towards an Integrated Framework for Violence Reduction* (London: Overseas Development Institute, 2002), https://www.odi.org/sites/odi.org.uk/files/odi-assets/publications-opinion-files/1826.pdf.

7. For example, Raymond Gilpin cites the work of Johan Galtung for the proposition that countries need "to make strategic investments that promote peace, equity, and welfare rather than focusing on prosecuting and stopping wars." Gilpin, "Peace Economics in a Changing World," *Economics of Peace and Security Journal* 12, no. 2 (2017): 32. See also "Policymaking Premises for Effective Economic Reconstruction" in del Castillo, *Obstacles to Peacebuilding*, 148–162.

8. Andrews, Pritchett, and Woolcock, *Escaping Capability Traps through Problem-Driven, Iterative Adaptation*, 21. See also "The Doing Development Differently Manifesto," http://doingdevelopmentdifferently.com/the-ddd-manifesto; Matt Andrews, Lant Pritchett, and Michael Woolcock, *Building State Capability: Evidence, Analysis, Action* (Oxford: Oxford University Press, 2017).

of knowledge, largely reflected in the efforts of various organizations and countries to develop more effective policies and strategies, have been described in the preceding discussion of what we have learned and elsewhere throughout this report.

The study group's recommended approach was a framework that would be "strategic, systemic, selective, and sustainable." These four principles have relevance not just for the United States but also for the broader international community.

1. Strategic
   - Prevent or mitigate future crises by identifying and addressing sources of fragility before they boil over into conflict and instability.
   - Couple prevention with resilience by investing in states and societies with the will and potential to respond to internal or external shocks.
   - Be rigorous about trade-offs between long-term objectives and short-term actions that risk undercutting strategic aims.
   - Strengthen international partnerships that promote openness and transparency.

2. Systemic
   - Develop a more proactive, adaptive, and synchronized interagency policy-planning and implementation process.
   - Foster an awareness of unintended consequences caused by interventions that focus on only one dynamic within a broader system.
   - Work toward a shared understanding among interagency actors.

3. Selective
   - Identify the most effective sources of external leverage to incentivize change.
   - Play to complementary strengths of international partners to avoid duplication of efforts.
   - Align interests and actions of international actors with local aspirations and solutions.
   - Work together where interests align, but do not overlook divergence.

4. Sustained
   - Avoid getting involved too late and leaving too early.
   - Structure realistic, flexible, and politically feasible plans.
   - Invest in success by making sure partners pursuing reforms receive support and assistance.
   - Avoid the trap of maximalist goals on unrealistic timelines.[9]

---

9. Burns, Flournoy, and Lindborg, *U.S. Leadership and the Challenge of State Fragility*, 12–13. To emphasize the broad relevance of these principles, the summary description of the four principles above refers generally to international actors in some places where the original refers specifically to the United States.

The Fragility Study Group organized its recommendations for priority actions by reference to three kinds of relationships: (i) domestic relationships among concerned public and private entities within a single international partner of fragile states, (ii) relationships among international partners of fragile states, and (iii) relationships by international partners with fragile states.[10] A similar framework is used below to present some ideas that might contribute to effective strategies, but without the references to "fragile states" found in the study group report. The study group addressed these relationships from a U.S. perspective. The following discussion, instead, addresses them from a broad global perspective. Implications for U.S. policy and practice are discussed in the following section.

Internal Relationships for an International Partner

Any country or multilateral organization seeking to engage in fragile situations will confront challenges due to differences among its own participating public entities and related private-sector and civil society organizations. To meet this challenge, it is necessary to have an internal system that is conducive to a collaborative, whole-of-government/whole-of-society approach.

Such a system should produce greater clarity in the formulation of context-specific policy objectives and in the division of labor for pursuing those objectives. This may require strengthening the geographic and subject-matter expertise and language skills of officials so they will be better able to provide continuity to long-term efforts, familiarity by the participating entities with interagency relationships and processes, and deep understanding of local conditions in the situation being addressed. Mechanisms should be developed to support longer tours of duty, career development, and cross-agency staff assignments.

The system for managing internal relationships also should empower a convening authority to facilitate transparent communication and shared understanding, guide coordinated adaptation by participating entities to changing circumstances, foster policy coherence, maintain discipline and focus in implementation, and resolve issues and disputes that may arise.

There will be need for flexible budget authority so that investments can be timely, aligned with identified local priorities, and sustained throughout the anticipated time of need. Effective prevention means that resources will be available before the crisis occurs; the time frame for institutional reform and societal transformation requires that resources continue to be available for an extended period.

Obtaining timely, sufficient, flexible, and consistent financing will depend upon political and public awareness, understanding, and support. Efforts will be needed to increase understanding of the dangers of inaction, appreciation of the complex nature of each fragile situation, and awareness of the likely time frame for expecting progress toward long-term objectives. Timely and transparent reporting on actions taken, resources committed, obstacles encountered, and progress achieved will be important to sustain credibility and confidence.

---

10. Ibid., 18–26.

Relationships among International Partners

A good starting point for improving international coordination would be to strengthen the consensus on those issues about which there is already substantial agreement. It would help to engage the international community broadly on issues such as viewing fragility as a continuum; reinforcing the emphasis on prevention; formulating and implementing integrated approaches that embrace the distinctive security, political, and development characteristics of each individual fragile situation; and preserving inclusive local ownership accompanied by strengthened mutual accountability.

Opportunities for engagement and consensus strengthening on these themes on a global scale will be provided by the 2018 high-level meeting of the UN General Assembly on Sustaining Peace and in the 2019 review of the implementation of SDG 16 in the High-Level Political Forum on Sustainable Development (HLPF). Synergies between the 2030 Agenda for Sustainable Development and the theme of sustaining peace were the subject of a high-level dialogue in the UN General Assembly in January 2017. The outcome of that dialogue will provide background for high-level deliberations both in the General Assembly and in the HLPF.[11]

The president of the 72nd session of the General Assembly has indicated his intention to give priority to the issues of prevention and mediation in sustaining peace. The high-level meeting on this theme at which he will preside has been scheduled for April 2018. According to the UN Sustainable Development Knowledge Platform, Goal 16 will be reviewed in depth in the HLPF in July 2019. The forum will meet that year at the level of heads of state and government under the auspices of the General Assembly. (It meets at that elevated level once in every four years.)

Revitalization and strengthening of the New Deal for Engagement in Fragile States provides another important opportunity for building consensus and coordinating efforts. The New Deal combines broad goals with an implementation approach that combines country self-assessments, flexible national plans, compacts to coordinate and harmonize support, and measures to promote trust while strengthening capacities. It is a highly credible framework for providing coordinated international support for efforts by countries to overcome the challenges of fragility and build resilient societies. Leadership by the 20 members of the g7+ provides a valuable perspective, and the broad participation of governments and organizations in the IDPS provides a critical mass for scaled-up efforts.

The independent review of the New Deal in 2016 by the Center for International Cooperation at New York University and the 2016 renewed commitment by IDPS members, discussed in Chapter 3, provide a solid basis for renewal and strengthening of this important instrument. The international community should seize the opportunity to streamline the New Deal mechanism and broaden participation, beginning with several strategically selected situations. These efforts should place emphasis on all the New Deal goals (political, security, justice, economic, and management

---

11. See UN, *Summary of Key Messages and Observations from the High-Level Dialogue on "Building Sustainable Peace for All: Synergies between the 2030 Agenda for Sustainable Development and Sustaining Peace"* (New York: UN, 2017a), http://www.un.org/pga/71/wp-content/uploads/sites/40/2015/08/Summary-of-the-High-level-Dialogue-on -Building-Sustainable-Peace-for-All.pdf.

of revenues and service delivery) and should include instruments of cooperation beyond the aid relationships that had been the original focus.

The biggest challenge to coherence will be in country-specific implementation. A reinvigorated New Deal will need to shape implementation responsibilities in ways compatible with local capabilities, political settlements, security conditions, and economic constraints and opportunities. In each situation, the New Deal should incentivize sustained political commitment and mutual accountability for results.

Perhaps lead international actors could be identified to work with local national entities on individual country compacts. These lead actors could help to improve coordination and coherence in implementation. This would be consistent with the recommendation of the Fragility Study Group that the United States should focus on "cases where U.S. interests and leverage are greatest" while empowering others to lead "where they have greater stakes and influence."[12]

More sharply focused analysis and streamlined compacts should concentrate on what are identified as the most urgent and important issues, addressing gaps in capacity, security, and legitimacy. They should distinguish between needs for knowledge and resources and needs for political commitment. Where improved governance is central to addressing fragility, compacts should address issues of participation, incentives, and preferences and beliefs that can enable sustained political commitment. Such focused, politically sensitive, and results-oriented compacts could help to overcome the stalled progress seen in a number of past New Deal initiatives.

Relationships with Countries Experiencing Fragility

Unquestionably, countries with fragile situations need to be full participants in deliberations on the issues described in the preceding paragraphs. The success of efforts within the UN system and in the New Deal will require broad support from the international community and must provide opportunities for the most directly affected members of that community, countries with fragile situations, to help shape the outcome. Beyond that, there are several specific measures in which those countries will be the principal actors.

Dialogue between local and international actors should address the complexity of fragility—its multiple dimensions, its long-term implications, and the need to address it in national strategies. International partners wishing to support national strategies should maintain their focus on key local priorities while being prepared to rely on varied kinds of support and engagement appropriate to the particular situation beyond the traditional instrument of development assistance.

Compacts might include, as appropriate to the local context, measures such as diplomatic dialogue on specific issues, educational and cultural exchanges, trade and investment relationships, private-sector business development, civil society oversight of government performance, and engagement with the security sector. Such multifaceted relationships, focused on carefully

---

12. Burns, Flournoy, and Lindborg, *U.S. Leadership and the Challenge of State Fragility*, 13. See also Albertson and Moran, *Untangling the Complexity of Fragile States*, 6.

selected priorities and with appropriate sequencing, can help overcome obstacles, provide incentives for sustained commitment, and build mutual confidence.

Where limited local capacity is an obstacle to progress, another way to sustain momentum and build mutual confidence is to consider collaborative arrangements for international actors to participate directly in implementation activities. Such participation, implemented with mutual respect, can help local actors to demonstrate success in implementing locally owned reforms in environments where they may face internal opposition.

Successful examples of direct international participation in national efforts include the joint assessments of constraints under the U.S.-led Partnership for Growth program; the UN-supported International Commission against Impunity in Guatemala (CICIG) that, in addition to capacity strengthening, provides international experts to investigate and assist in local prosecution in high-level corruption cases; and Liberia's multiparty partnership for governance and economic management (GEMAP).[13]

The stubbornly resistant fragile situation is the most challenging. When resistance is due more to weak legitimacy than to limited capacity, financial and technical assistance alone cannot be expected to produce change. Authoritarian leaders and entrenched elites typically want to preserve their privileged positions. As the *WDR* 2017 reminds, the response needs to address such power asymmetries through efforts to change contestability, provide incentives, and influence preferences and beliefs. These situations demand focused strategies that are individually tailored to each local situation, whole-of-government approaches, and coordination among committed national and international actors.[14]

As contemplated in the EU Global Strategy described in Chapter 3, it may be appropriate in some change-resistant situations to consider withholding support other than humanitarian relief, organizing joint diplomatic overtures, or in extreme cases, imposing international sanctions on corrupt or criminal local actors. Even in such cases, a strategy might include both sanctions and

---

13. For Partnership for Growth, see Department of State (2014), "Mid-Term Evaluation: Partnership for Growth, El Salvador—United States," https://www.state.gov/f/evaluations/all/233959.htm. For Guatemala CICIG, see the CICIG website, http://www.cicig.org. For Liberia GEMAP, see Kemp Ronald Hope, "Liberia's Governance and Economic Management Assistance Program (GEMAP): An Impact Review and Analytical Assessment of a Donor Policy Intervention for Democratic State-Building in a Post-Conflict State," *South African Journal of International Affairs* 17, no. 2 (2010): 243–263, https://www.researchgate.net/publication/233208364_Liberia%27s_Governance_and_Economic_Management_Assistance_Program_GEMAP_an_impact_review_and_analytical_assessment_of_a_donor_policy_intervention_for_democratic_state-building_in_a_post-conflict_state. See also the examples of specialized criminal justice mechanisms, often involving international participation, summarized in chapter 4 of Colette Rausch, ed., *Fighting Serious Crimes: Strategies and Tactics for Conflict-Affected Societies* (Washington, DC: U.S. Institute of Peace, 2017), 106–168.

14. An example is the response to repeated efforts by Guatemalan political leaders to undermine the investigative work of national prosecutors collaborating with CICIG. See, for example, "Prosecutors Target Guatemalan President over Campaign Financing," Reuters World News, August 25, 2017, https://www.reuters.com/article/us-guatemala-corruption-idUSKCN1B52R8; "If You Elect a Clown, Expect a Circus," *Economist*, September 2–8, 2017. Despite the controversy, the government of Guatemala and the United Nations have agreed on an extension of the CICIG mandate for an additional two years (until September 2019). See also H. Res. 145, 115th Congress, https://www.congress.gov/115/bills/hres145/BILLS-115hres145eh.pdf, expressing support for CICIG and other anticorruption initiatives.

selective support to individuals and organizations. Libya and Somalia provide examples where both sanctions and selective support are simultaneously operational.[15]

INNOVATIVE THINKING FOR EFFECTIVE STRATEGIES

In addition to building on what we have learned and strengthening relationships among national and international actors, innovative thinking will be important to achieving more effective strategies. Integration of the creative ideas described in Chapter 3 can provide several ways to enhance the value of collaborative international engagement. In particular,

Pauline Baker identified a limited number of principal factors that have contributed to the deterioration as well as to the restoration of stability and resilience. Her analysis suggests how national strategies and international support can be shaped in order to concentrate on the most likely impediments to progress.

Michael Crosswell distinguished between obstacles that can benefit from international support for capacity strengthening and those where priority attention needs to be on achieving a political context supportive of sustained commitment. This demonstrates the need to look beyond the typical emphasis on providing aid for capacity building. The *WDR* 2017 recommends ways to overcome asymmetries in the balance of power among key actors so that the local political context will be accepting of the necessary sustained commitment.

Charles Call recommended that attention be given to related gaps in capacity, security, and legitimacy, together with sensitivity to the need for balancing these factors in a coherent response. His insight highlights the need for coordinated and sophisticated strategies that look at the interrelationships among issues. Anthony Bell and his colleagues provide illustrations of how Call's analytical framework can help to align security, humanitarian, and development elements of international engagement.

J. Eli Margolis, in offering a variation on gap analysis, provides another important insight: as deterioration increases in the realms of state authority, resilience, and legitimacy, there is also an increased risk that relatively minor incidents will become progressively more capable of triggering a crisis. One aspect of prevention, therefore, is to be alert to potential triggers.

Taking advantage of technology is another aspect of innovation that can help to shape more effective strategies. Strategy formulation should consider initiatives like the PeaceTech Lab, which seeks to bring together technology, media, and data to accelerate the development of solutions, distribute them faster, and engage more people.[16]

---

15. See, with respect to Libya, UN, "List Established and Maintained Pursuant to Security Council Res. 1970 (2011)" (Libya sanctions), https://scsanctions.un.org/fop/fop?xml=htdocs/resources/xml/en/consolidated.xml&xslt=htdocs /resources/xsl/en/libya.xsl; USAID Libya Country Profile website, https://www.usaid.gov/libya/fact-sheets/country -profile. With respect to Somalia, see UN, "Somalia: Sanctions Measures," https://www.un.org/sc/suborg/en/sanctions /751#Somalia; USAID, "Somalia," https://www.usaid.gov/somalia; and USAID, "Food Assistance Fact Sheet—Somalia," https://www.usaid.gov/somalia/food-assistance.

16. See the PeaceTech Lab website, http://www.peacetechlab.org.

PRIORITIZING THE PREVENTION OF FRAGILITY

As we have learned more about fragility, often by trial and error, we have come to recognize it as a threat to both security and development. We have identified ways to contain and mitigate its harmful consequences. International networks have collaborated to harmonize their approaches and develop common guidance, including calls for preventive strategies and integration of efforts.

But, as is so often the case with complex issues that have uncertain near-term outcomes, there is a persistent gap between knowledge and action. The predominant international response to fragility, in fact, has been reactive rather than proactive. Circumstances continue to overtake the coping capabilities of countries like South Sudan and Yemen. Insecure, dispossessed, and impoverished people living precariously in fragile situations continue to seek safety and opportunity elsewhere. Criminal and terrorist elements are finding safe haven in poorly governed places. This continuing gap between knowledge and action defies logic, exacerbates risks, and imposes unnecessary and, for some, tragic costs. Unchecked continuation of present trends will lead to more tragedies affecting more people. This is unsustainable.

Ultimately, more effective, integrated strategies that emphasize prevention will have to emerge from a widely shared conviction that fragility can be contained and reversed, that timely and sustained international action can have a positive influence, and that the effort this implies is worthwhile. Achieving such a shared conviction will require a fundamental elevation of public awareness, supported by committed political leadership, in countries experiencing fragility as well as in the many countries affected by it throughout the world.

The UN secretary-general's initiative "to persuade decision makers at both the national and international levels to make prevention their priority," discussed in Chapter 3, could be an opportune channel for elevating awareness and encouraging leadership. The reinvigoration of the New Deal is an opportunity to demonstrate that committed local efforts and enlightened international influence and support can change the dangerous trajectory that fragile situations too often present. These opportunities should not be missed.

IMPLICATIONS FOR THE UNITED STATES

The ideas presented above for improving the international response to fragility draw on many sources of learning and experience. A common characteristic is that they can be given practical effect only through the efforts of many actors. The following discussion draws on international learning and experience to recommend ways for the United States to improve its effectiveness in managing fragility and promoting transitions to resilience.

To begin, the Fragility Study Group's suggestion of a framework that is strategic, systemic, selective, and sustained is highly commendable. Within that framework, the following measures should be considered:

1. Abandon the binary approach that treats some states as fragile and others as not fragile. Instead, recognize that fragility is a multidimensional continuum affecting many countries and bring fragility considerations into the mainstream of international relations.

Treating fragility as a condition that affects only a relatively few countries and focusing on the most severe situations has two major shortcomings. This approach gives inadequate attention to the dozens of countries that are experiencing challenges in one or more dimensions of fragility that merit early attention. At the same time, a binary approach, by treating countries experiencing fragility as "different," tends to give a prominent role to agencies, offices, and personnel that deal with a specialized subject on a global basis. This necessarily diminishes the role of those who have greater depth of regional and country-specific knowledge and expertise and who have primary responsibility for managing relations with the countries and regions of concern.

Of course, repositories of specialized knowledge are needed, with expertise such as that found in the Department of State's Bureau of Conflict and Stabilization, USAID's Office of Conflict Mitigation and Management, and the Defense Department's Peacekeeping and Stability Operations Unit. However, these specialized offices should supplement and not replace normal channels for diplomacy, development, and security cooperation.

The benefit of integrating an issue in the policy mainstream is demonstrated by the experience of the Department of State in the treatment of human rights issues and the experience of USAID in addressing gender equality and public-private partnerships. These experiences show that mainstreaming is conducive to reliance on approaches that are integral to U.S. policy and that are context appropriate. Such approaches are essential for responding effectively to fragility.

Some instances of weak institutional capacity, social cohesion, and legitimacy of governance will be of only minor significance for U.S. international interests. In other situations, these issues will be of greater concern and will have varying significance in the shaping and implementation of U.S. policy. The facts and interests of each case should determine the ways in which fragility issues influence policy and programs.

2. Strengthen and streamline coordination mechanisms to minimize fragmentation, facilitate efficiency, and maximize coherence of efforts.

International engagement on fragility issues involves dealing with interrelated political, security, and development aspects of fragile situations. However, U.S. agency responsibilities are not always clear and frequently overlap. Actions are not always consistent.

There should be an arrangement, explicitly directed by the National Security Council (NSC), that authorizes the Department of State to exercise overall political coordination. Under the Department of State's leadership, USAID should be designated to coordinate on development issues and the Department of Defense to coordinate on security issues. Other agencies should be included to deal with particular issues within their expertise: for example, the Treasury Department on engagement with multilateral development banks and the Commerce Department on trade.

Major policy issues will surely require monitoring, deliberations, and periodic review at senior levels in the NSC system. However, empowering the agencies to operate in a coordinated way on a day-to-day basis should help to build understanding and collaborative relationships and overcome bureaucratic cultural differences while also reducing the complications and inefficiencies of waiting for prior NSC approval of actions needed to implement approved policies.

3. Build expertise in the multiple dimensions of fragility into the human resource base of the concerned agencies, including incentives for longer assignments and language proficiency, expanded training opportunities, and career development rewards.

If fragility is treated as a mainstream issue, it should be increasingly feasible to build a cadre of staff possessing the necessary skills and knowledge and prepared to commit to lengthy assignments consistent with the time frame in which results can reasonably be expected. Consistent with the mainstreaming objective, a significant number of these skilled individuals, when assigned to headquarters positions, should be integrated in the staffs of operating bureaus and offices, not isolated in "fragility specialist" enclaves.

4. Increase emphasis on early warning and early responses that can help to prevent deterioration of fragile situations into crisis or conflict.

The United States should establish a fragility early warning system, building on the work of the Political Instability Task Force described in Chapter 3. The system would collect and disseminate to the interagency community information on countries that are experiencing economic, environmental, political, security, or societal fragility. This would alert policymakers to vulnerable situations where early preventive measures might be warranted.

A fragility early warning system of the U.S. government should not duplicate the annual reviews of country situations that are published by the World Bank, the OECD, the FFP, and others. Rather than serve as a vehicle for public naming and shaming, the system should be a reliable predictor of change for the benefit of policymakers. Those who receive the system's reporting can decide on what, if any, action is needed, including any need for publicity.

As previously noted, one benefit of an early warning system would be to have a body of information for engaging Congress and public opinion on the virtue of preventive measures intended to avoid a later need for more costly efforts in a potentially more dangerous and uncertain environment. Reliable reporting from the system could also be of use when engaging the international community. But when and how to publicize reporting from the early warning system should be a decision of policymakers, not a routine function of the system.

The early warning system could be modeled after the successful Famine Early Warning System (FEWS), long managed by USAID. Given USAID's positive experience with FEWS and that agency's general project management capabilities, USAID would seem a likely candidate to manage the fragility early warning system. USAID management of the system should include continuous communication and consultation to ensure that it is responsive to the needs of all concerned agencies.

Selectivity is one of the principles of the Fragility Study Group's proposed framework for U.S. policy. As previously noted, some situations will not require action and sometimes other international actors will be better situated to take the lead. However, having a systematic approach for early warning will facilitate timely decisions about what U.S. political, development, or security response, if any, is appropriate.

5. Provide leadership through actions to strengthen the international response to fragility.

The response to the complex threat that fragility poses to peace, security, and sustainable development is an international responsibility. The United States can exercise its leadership to help to shape that international response so as to make the most of the contributions of all concerned countries and organizations.

The revitalization of the New Deal pursuant to the 2016 Stockholm Declaration provides an opportunity for the United States to take the lead in specific cases to introduce more sharply focused and streamlined implementation and innovative approaches within the New Deal framework. These initiatives would direct integrated, context-appropriate efforts at the various security, political, and economic aspects of each situation along the lines suggested above in this chapter.

The positive U.S. experience with the compact approach developed by the MCC is well known internationally. The experience provides a solid foundation for U.S. leadership in New Deal revitalization. It can be adapted in ways compatible with more fragile situations than just those where MCC operates. Several ideas on how to do this are described in Chapter 3. U.S. leadership could help to make the New Deal compact approach a more effective instrument for addressing—on the basis of mutual accountability—the broad range of economic, political, and security challenges that are often magnified in fragile situations.

Among the countries already engaged in New Deal implementation are Afghanistan, Haiti, Liberia, and Somalia, all countries where the United States has a long-standing and continuing major involvement. U.S. leadership to help shape New Deal implementation in one or more of these countries could be accompanied by a U.S. supporting role in one or more countries where another international actor is in the lead.

A second area of opportunity is to engage with the multilateral development institutions on rationalizing their approach to fragility. The World Bank, the IMF, and the regional development banks all have sophisticated understandings of the complexities of fragility and the need for interdisciplinary responses. However, their operational flexibility is constrained by the persistence of policies related to the Harmonized List, which treat certain low-income countries and countries with a peacekeeping or peacebuilding presence under different policies than other fragile situations. Active dialogue with staffs and directors of these institutions should encourage greater flexibility and improved integration of their programs with other international efforts.

A major third opportunity for U.S. leadership is the UN secretary-general's initiative to "connect global efforts for peace and security, sustainable development and human rights" and "to persuade decision-makers . . . to make prevention their priority." This initiative will be given content in the secretary-general's report in advance of the April 2018 high-level meeting of the UN General Assembly on strengthening the work of the United Nations on sustaining peace. A leading and supportive U.S. engagement in the evolution of this initiative could advance the general U.S. interest in increasing the effectiveness of the United Nations and the many organizations with which it works. The United States should also facilitate the important objectives of integrating the various components of the international response to fragility and prioritizing prevention as a leading principle in that response.

CONCLUSIONS

This chapter has reviewed the complexities, variety of manifestations, and divergent perspectives that combine to impede a coherent and consistent international response to fragility. It recalls the many lessons learned about how these impediments might be overcome. These include the value of context-specific, focused approaches that are informed by early warning systems, oriented to timely preventive action, and implemented in a coordinated manner.

On this basis, the chapter proposes ways to make international responses more strategic, systemic, selective, and sustained. It advocates structures for improving coordination within international actor organizations, among international actors, and with societies that are experiencing fragility. And it calls attention to opportunities for innovative thinking and the importance of prevention.

Finally, the chapter offers specific ideas about the potential role for the United States—in improving the effectiveness of its own efforts and also in exercising international leadership.

Ultimately, more effective strategies to diminish fragility and promote resilience will depend upon the readiness of political leaders and concerned citizens to act in coordinated ways to put into practice the lessons learned about fragility. This implies a willingness to work together at a time when a variety of centrifugal forces seem to be pulling at the cohesion and solidarity of many communities, countries, and regions throughout the world.

Overall Conclusions

This report has recounted how fragility has become a significant global challenge. It places the threats to security and development posed by fragility in the context of centuries-long trends toward declining violence and increased prosperity and freedom, trends that have been integral aspects of gradual improvement in the quality of life throughout the world. And it shows how today's fragile situations represent exceptions to these historic global trends—and potential threats to their continuation.

The tendency of countries experiencing fragility to combine stagnant or shrinking economies, high levels of poverty and inequality, and rapidly growing populations is antithetical to sustainable development. The tendency of fragile environments to experience disproportionate levels of popular grievance, conflict, organized criminal violence, and terrorist acts beyond the control of local authorities threatens peace and security. The negative influences of poverty and violence are mutually reinforcing.

The people who live in these situations will be the most directly and severely affected by failure to meet the international pledge "that no-one will be left behind."[1] In some cases, economic, environmental, and societal fragility have undermined regional as well as national prosperity and stability. In other cases, prolonged violence and corruption have diminished security, impeded accountable and effective governance, and enabled criminal and terrorist organizations to extend their violent acts and recruitment beyond national borders to threaten other countries and their citizens.

Governments, public and private international organizations, multilateral development banks, private business organizations, and civil society groups have all struggled with the multiple and interrelated challenges of fragility. These stakeholders have adopted policies and strategies, reviewed their implementation experience, and then repeatedly revised and refined their previous policies and strategies. They have worked to improve coordination among international actors who bring differing perspectives to the effort and they have come to share many judgments:

---

1. UN, *Transforming Our World*, preamble and para. 4.

Fragility manifests itself in different ways and with varying severity in different national and regional contexts. It is necessary in any given situation to recognize that each of the dimensions of fragility—economic, environmental, political, security, and societal—is at some point along a continuum ranging from crisis to resilience.

There are no generalized solutions to achieve transitions from crisis and instability to resilience and peaceful development. Each fragile situation presents a distinct challenge which needs to be met by efforts that are compatible with the local context.

International engagement needs to be timely and sustained in order to head off disintegration into crisis and diminish risks of regression. It needs to foster local commitment and capabilities, support incentives and beliefs conducive to enhanced self-reliance, and continue long enough so that progress can be sustained. International actors cannot impose their solutions, but need to be respectful of local sovereignty and local knowledge in a spirit of collaboration while building mutual trust and accountability.

Innovative thought leaders have brought to our attention promising insights and creative ideas for improving the international response. These include seeking to identify and focus on key drivers of fragility; considering tensions among gaps in capacity, security, and legitimacy; distinguishing between needs for knowledge and resources and needs for conditions that will facilitate political commitment; and being alert to the risk of events that can trigger instability in situations of diminished authority, resilience, and legitimacy. In addition, thoughtful studies have identified how capabilities and strategies can be strengthened and how relationships among national and international actors can be made more productive and coherent.

The significant risks and negative consequences of fragility are evident. Coordinated international efforts to mitigate the risks and prevent the negative consequences are clearly preferable to being surprised by each new crisis and reacting to it. Each fragile situation that is ameliorated will reduce risks, avoid the need for more costly and less promising reactive efforts after a crisis occurs, and perhaps help to establish a pattern of collaborative behavior that can be extended to other areas of common endeavor.

It is clear that only a broadly shared political commitment and coordinated international action will be able to manage the threat to security and development posed by fragility. As in the case of other complex issues with multiple stakeholders and diverse interests, such a response will be very hard to achieve. As stated in the Introduction, the purpose of this report has been to stimulate thinking and action by political leaders, public and private organizations, and citizens. The author's hopeful expectation is that the information and ideas presented here will be useful in advocacy for policies and programs to support durable resolutions of existing conflicts, help prevent fragile situations from deteriorating into future crises, and foster more resilient societies, thereby advancing peace, security, and sustainable development.

Selected Bibliography

Accra Agenda for Action. 2008. Tunis: African Development Bank. https://www.afdb.org/fileadmin/uploads /afdb/Documents/AccraAgendaAaction-4sept2008-FINAL-ENG_16h00.pdf.

Acemoglu, Daron. 2008. "Interactions between Governance and Growth." In *Governance, Growth, and Development Decision-making*, by Douglass North, Daron Acemoglu, Francis Fukuyama, and Dani Rodrik, 1–8. Washington, DC: World Bank. http://siteresources.worldbank.org/EXTPUBLICSECTORAND GOVERNANCE/Resources/governanceandgrowth.pdf.

Acemoglu, Daron, and James Robinson. 2012. *Why Nations Fail: The Origins of Power, Prosperity, and Poverty.* New York: Crown Books.

Adams, Tani Marilena. 2017. *How Chronic Violence Affects Human Development, Social Relations, and the Practice of Citizenship.* Washington, DC: Woodrow Wilson Center. https://www.wilsoncenter.org /publication/how-chronic-violence-affects-human-development-social-relations-and-the-practice.

African Development Bank (AfDB). 2001. *Post-Conflict Policy Guidelines.* Abidjan: AfDB. https://www.afdb .org/fileadmin/uploads/afdb/Documents/Policy-Documents/32%20-EN%20-Bank_Group_Post-conflict _Assistance_Policy_Guidelines_-_Revised_%28Approval%29_01.pdf.

——. 2008. *Strategy for Enhanced Engagement in Fragile States.* Tunis: AfDB. https://www.afdb.org /fileadmin/uploads/afdb/Documents/Policy-Documents/30736191-EN-STRATEGY-FOR-ENHANCED -ENGAGEMENT-IN-FRAGILES-STATES.PDF.

——. 2012. *Development Effectiveness Review 2012—Fragile States and Conflict-Affected Countries.* Tunis: AfDB. https://www.afdb.org/fileadmin/uploads/afdb/Documents/Project-and-Operations/Development _Effectiveness_Review_2012_-_Fragile_States_and_Conflict-Affected_Countries.pdf.

——. 2014a. *African Development Bank Group Strategy for Addressing Fragility and Building Resilience in Africa.* Abidjan: AfDB. https://www.afdb.org/fileadmin/uploads/afdb/Documents/Policy-Documents/Addressing _Fragility_and_Building_Resilience_in_Africa-_The_AfDB_Group_Strategy_2014%E2%80%932019.pdf.

——. 2014b. *Ending Conflict and Building Peace in Africa: A Call to Action.* Abidjan: AfDB. https://www.afdb .org/fileadmin/uploads/afdb/Documents/Project-and-Operations/Ending_Conflict_and_Building _Peace_in_Africa-_A_Call_to_Action.pdf.

———. 2014c. *Operational Guidelines for the Implementation of the Strategy for Addressing Fragility and Building Resilience in Africa and for the Transition Support Facility.* Abidjan: AfDB. https://www .afdb.org/fileadmin/uploads/afdb/Documents/Policy-Documents/Operational_Guidelines_for_the _Implementation_of_the_Strategy_for_addressing_Fragility_and_building_Resilience_in_Africa_and _for_TSF_-APPROVED.pdf.

African Development Bank, Asian Development Bank, European Bank for Reconstruction and Development, European Investment Bank, Inter-American Development Bank, International Monetary Fund, and World Bank. 2015. *From Billions to Trillions: Transforming Development Finance—Post-2015 Financing for Development: Multilateral Development Finance.* Development Committee Discussion Note. Washington, DC: World Bank. http://siteresources.worldbank.org/DEVCOMMINT/Documentation/23659446 /DC2015-0002(E)FinancingforDevelopment.pdf.

Albertson, Andrew, and Ashley Moran. 2016. *A Call for a New Strategic Approach to Fragile States.* Washington, DC: Truman Center. http://trumancenter.org/wp-content/uploads/2011/07/A-Call-for-a-New -Strategic-Approach-to-Fragile-States.pdf.

———. 2017. *Untangling the Complexity of Fragile States.* Washington, DC: Truman Center. http:// trumancenter.org/wp-content/uploads/2017/03/Untangling-the-Complexity-of-Fragile-States.pdf.

Alkire, Sabina. 2010. "Human Development: Definitions, Critiques, and Related Concepts." OPHI Working Paper 36, University of Oxford. http://www.ophi.org.uk/wp-content/uploads/OPHI_WP36.pdf.

Anderson, G. Willian. 2014. "Bridging the Divide: How Can USAID and DoD Integrate Security and Development More Effectively in Africa?" *Fletcher Forum of World Affairs* 38 (1): 101–126.

Andrews, Matt, Lant Pritchett, and Michael Woolcock. 2012. *Escaping Capability Traps through Problem-Driven Iterative Adaptation.* Center for Global Development Working Paper 299, Center for Global Development, Washington, DC. http://www.cgdev.org/sites/default/files/1426292_file_Andrews _Pritchett_Woolcock_traps_FINAL_0.pdf.

———. 2017. *Building State Capability: Evidence, Analysis, Action.* Oxford: Oxford University Press.

Asian Development Bank (ADB). 2007. *Achieving Development in Weakly Performing Countries (The Asian Development Bank's Approach to Engaging with Weakly Performing Countries).* Manila: ADB. https:// www.adb.org/sites/default/files/institutional-document/32039/secm30-07.pdf.

———. 2010a. *Special Evaluation Study: Asian Development Bank's Support to Fragile and Conflict-Affected Situations.* Manila: ADB. https://www.oecd.org/derec/adb/47186709.pdf.

———. 2010b. *Management Response to the Special Evaluation Study.* Manila: ADB. https://www.adb.org /sites/default/files/institutional-document/33219/files/mr-ses-reg-2010-45.pdf.

———. 2010c. *ADB Engagement in Fragile and Conflict-Affected Situations, 2007–2009.* Manila: ADB. https:// www.adb.org/sites/default/files/page/59522/session-5-fragile-conflict-affected-situations.pdf.

———. 2012. *Working Differently in Fragile and Conflict-Affected Situations—The ADB Experience: A Staff Handbook.* Manila: ADB. https://www.adb.org/sites/default/files/institutional-document/33774/files /working-differently-conflict-affected-situations.pdf.

———. 2013. *Operational Plan for Enhancing ADB's Effectiveness in Fragile and Conflict-Affected Situations.* Manila: ADB. https://www.adb.org/sites/default/files/institutional-document/33825/files/operational -plan-fcas.pdf.

——. 2014. *Fragility Index for a Differentiated Approach*. Manila: ADB. https://www.adb.org/sites/default/files/publication/42814/fragility-index-differentiated-approach-fcas.pdf.

Avis, William Robert. 2016. *Private Sector Engagement in Fragile and Conflict-Affected Settings*. Birmingham: Governance and Social Development Research Centre (GSDRC). http://www.gsdrcd.org/wp-content/uploads/2016/03/HDQ1331.pdf.

Baker, Pauline H. 2017. *Reframing State Fragility and Resilience: The Way Forward*. Washington, DC: Creative Associates International. http://www.creativeassociatesinternational.com/wp-content/uploads/2017/02/Reframing_Way_Foward.pdf.

Bell, Anthony, Kathryn McNabb Cochran, Melissa Dalton, Marc Frey, Alice Hunt Friend, Rebecca K. C. Hersman, and Sarah Minot. 2017. *Meeting Security Challenges in a Disordered World*. Washington, DC: Center for Strategic and International Studies (CSIS). https://www.csis.org/analysis/meeting-security-challenges-disordered-world.

Besley, Timothy, and Torsten Persson. 2011a. *Pillars of Prosperity: The Political Economics of Development Clusters*. Princeton, NJ: Princeton University Press.

——. 2011b. *Fragile States and Development Policy*. London: London School of Economics and Political Science. http://sticerd.lse.ac.uk/dps/eopp/eopp22.pdf.

Bhuta, Nehal. 2015. "Measuring Stateness, Ranking Political Orders: Indices of State Fragility and State Failure." In *Ranking the World: Grading States as a Tool of Global Governance*, edited by Alexander Cooley and Jack Snyder, 85-111. Cambridge: Cambridge University Press.

Bosetti, Louise, Alexandra Ivanovic, and Menaal Munshey. 2016. *Fragility, Risk, and Resilience: A Review of Existing Frameworks*. Tokyo: United Nations University. https://i.unu.edu/media/cpr.unu.edu/attachment/2232/Assessing-Fragility-Risk-and-Resilience-Frameworks.pdf.

Brinkerhoff, Derick. 2014. "State Fragility and Failure as Wicked Problems: Beyond Naming and Taming." *Third World Quarterly* 35 (2): 333–344.

Brown, David E. 2013. *AFRICOM at Five Years: The Maturation of a New U.S. Combatant Command*. Carlisle, PA: U.S. Army War College Press. https://ssi.armywarcollege.edu/pdffiles/PUB1164.pdf.

Burns, William, Michèle Flournoy, and Nancy Lindborg. 2016. *U.S. Leadership and the Challenge of State Fragility: Fragility Study Group Report*. Washington, DC: Carnegie Endowment for International Peace, Center for a New American Security, U.S. Institute of Peace. http://www.usip.org/fragility-report.

Burnside, Craig, and David Dollar. 2009. *Aid, Policies, and Growth*. Washington, DC: World Bank. http://documents.worldbank.org/curated/en/698901468739531893/pdf/multi-page.pdf.

Busan Conference. 2011. *Busan Partnership for Effective Development Cooperation*. Paris: OECD. http://www.oecd.org/development/effectiveness/49650173.pdf.

Cahill, Kevin M., ed. 2000. *Preventive Diplomacy: Stopping Wars before They Start*. New York: Routledge.

Call, Charles. 2008a. *Beyond the "Failed State": Seeking Conceptual Alternatives*. Paper presented at the International Studies Association Annual Meeting, San Francisco. http://citation.allacademic.com//meta/p_mla_apa_research_citation/2/5/4/3/2/pages254326/p254326-1.php.

——. 2008b. "The Fallacy of the 'Failed State.'" *Third World Quarterly* 29 (8): 1491–1507.

——. 2010. "Beyond the 'Failed State': Toward Conceptual Alternatives." *European Journal of International Relations* 17 (2): 303–326.

Cammack, Perry, Michele Dunne, Amr Hamzawy, Marc Lynch, Marwan Muasher, Yezid Sayigh, and Maha Yahya. 2017. *Arab Fractures: Citizens, States, and Social Contracts*. Washington, DC: Carnegie Endowment for International Peace. http://carnegieendowment.org/files/Arab_World_Horizons_Final.pdf.

Carment, David, Simon Langlois-Bertrand, and Yiagadeesen Samy. 2016. *Assessing State Fragility, with a Focus on Climate Change and Refugees*. Ottawa: Carleton University. http://www4.carleton.ca/cifp/app/serve.php/1530.pdf.

Carnegie Commission on Preventing Deadly Conflict. 1997. *Final Report: Preventing Deadly Conflict*. New York: Carnegie Corporation of New York. https://www.carnegie.org/media/filer_public/b2/0e/b20e1080-7830-4f2b-9410-51c14171809b/ccny_report_1997_ccpdc_final.pdf.

Carvalho, Soniya. 2006. *Engaging with Fragile States: An IEG Review of World Bank Support to Low-Income Countries under Stress*. Washington, DC: World Bank. http://documents.worldbank.org/curated/en/418191468142504861/pdf/382850Revised01gile0states01PUBLIC1.pdf.

Castillejo, Clare. 2015. *Fragile States: An Urgent Challenge for EU Foreign Policy*. Madrid: Fundación para las Relaciones Internacionales y el Diálogo. http://fride.org/download/WP126_Fragile_states.pdf.

Chandy, Laurence, Natasha Ledlie, and Veronika Penciakova. 2013. *The Final Countdown: Prospects for Ending Extreme Poverty by 2030*. Washington, DC: Brookings Institution. https://www.brookings.edu/wp-content/uploads/2016/06/The_Final_Countdown.pdf.

Chandy, Laurence, Brijna Seidel, and Christine Zhang. 2016. *Aid Effectiveness in Fragile States: How Bad Is It and How Can It Improve?* Washington, DC: Brookings Institution. https://www.brookings.edu/wp-content/uploads/2016/12/global_121616_brookeshearer.pdf.

Chioda, Laura. 2017. *Stop the Violence in Latin America: A Look at Prevention from Cradle to Adulthood*. Washington, DC: World Bank.

Commission on International Development. 1969. *Partners in Development*. New York: Praeger.

Commission on Weak States and U.S. National Security. 2004. *On the Brink: Weak States and the U.S. National Security*. Washington, DC: Center for Global Development.

Coomaraswamy, Radhika. 2015. *Preventing Conflict, Transforming Justice, Securing the Peace*. New York: UN Women. http://wps.unwomen.org/pdf/en/GlobalStudy_EN_Web.pdf.

Council of the European Union. 2007. *Council Conclusions on a EU Response to Situations of Fragility*. Brussels: Publications Office of the EU. https://europa.eu/capacity4dev/public-fragility/document/council-conclusions-eu-response-situations-fragility.

——. 2014. *Council Conclusions on the EU's Comprehensive Approach*. Brussels: Publications Office of the EU. https://europa.eu/capacity4dev/public-fragility/document/council-conclusions-eus-comprehensive-approach.

Crosswell, Michael J. 2010. *Governance, Development and Foreign Aid Policy*. Oxford: 2010 Oxford Business & Economics Conference Program. http://pdf.usaid.gov/pdf_docs/PBAAD523.pdf.

Datzberger, Simone, and Mike Denison. 2013. *Private Sector Development in Fragile States*. London: Economics and Private Sector–Professional Evidence and Applied Knowledge Services. https://assets

.publishing.service.gov.uk/media/57a08a2ced915d622c0005cf/Private_Sector_Development_in
_Fragile_States.pdf.

Deaton, Angus. 2013. *The Great Escape: Health, Wealth, and the Origins of Inequality.* Princeton, NJ: Princeton University Press.

de Bruijne, Kars. 2017. *Crises: Fragile States; Thematic Study, Clingendael Strategic Monitor 2017.* The Hague: Netherlands Institute of International Relations, 2017. https://www.clingendael.org/sites/default /files/pdfs/clingendael_strategic_monitor_2017_crises_fragile_states.pdf.

Del Biondo, Karen. 2014. *The EU, the US, and Partnership in Development Cooperation: Bridging the Gap?* Stanford, CA: Stanford Center on Democracy, Development and the Rule of Law. https://fsi.fsi.stanford .edu/sites/default/files/del_biondo_2_final.pdf.

del Castillo, Graciana. 2017. *Obstacles to Peacebuilding.* New York: Routledge.

Department for International Development (DFID). 2005. *Why We Need to Work More Effectively in Fragile States.* London: DFID. http://webarchive.nationalarchives.gov.uk/20050117000000/http://www.dfid.gov .uk/pubs/files/fragilestates-paper.pdf.

———. 2015. *UK Aid: Tackling Global Challenges in the National Interest.* London: DFID. https://www.gov.uk /government/uploads/system/uploads/attachment_data/file/478834/ODA_strategy_final_web_0905 .pdf.

Department of State. 2008. *Interagency Conflict Assessment Framework.* Washington, DC: Department of State. https://www.state.gov/documents/organization/187786.pdf.

———. 2017. *Country Reports on Terrorism 2016.* Washington, DC: Department of State. https://www.state .gov/documents/organization/272488.pdf.

Department of State and U.S. Agency for International Development. 2016. *Joint Strategy on Countering Violent Extremism.* Washington, DC: U.S. Agency for International Development (USAID). http://pdf.usaid .gov/pdf_docs/PBAAE503.pdf.

Department of State, Department of Defense, Agency for International Development. 2009. *U.S. Government Counterinsurgency Guide.* Washington, DC: Department of State. https://www.state.gov/docu ments/organization/119629.pdf.

de Soto, Álvaro, and Graciana del Castillo. 2016. "Obstacles to Peacebuilding Revisited." *Global Governance* 22 (2): 209–227.

Di Bella, José, Alicia Grant, Shannon Kindornay, and Stephanie Tissot. 2013. *Mapping Private Sector Engagements in Development Cooperation.* Ottawa: North-South Institute. http://www.nsi-ins.ca/wp -content/uploads/2013/09/Mapping-PS-Engagment-in-Development-Cooperation-Final.pdf.

Dollar, David, and Lant Pritchett. 1998. *Assessing Aid: What Works, What Doesn't, and Why.* New York: Oxford University Press. http://documents.worldbank.org/curated/en/612481468764422935/pdf/multi -page.pdf.

Dupuy, Kendra, Håvard Mokleiv Nygård, Ida Rudolfsen, Håvard Strand, and Henrik Urdal. 2016. *Trends in Armed Conflict, 1946–2015.* Oslo: Peace Research Institute Oslo. http://files.prio.org/Publication_files /prio/Dupuy%20et%20al%20-%20Trends%20in%20Armed%20Conflict%201946-2015,%20Conflict%20 Trends%208-2016.pdf.

European Commission. 2007. *Towards an EU Response to Situations of Fragility: Engaging in Difficult Environments for Sustainable Development, Stability and Peace.* Brussels: Publications Office of the EU. http://eur-lex.europa.eu/LexUriServ/LexUriServ.do?uri=COM:2007:0643:FIN:EN:PDF.

European Commission and High Representative of the European Union for Foreign Affairs and Security Policy. 2013. *The EU's Comprehensive Approach to External Conflict and Crises.* Brussels: Publications Office of the EU. http://www.eeas.europa.eu/archives/docs/statements/docs/2013/131211_03_en.pdf.

———. 2015. *Taking Forward the EU's Comprehensive Approach to External Conflict and Crises—Action Plan 2015.* Brussels: Publications Office of the EU. http://data.consilium.europa.eu/doc/document/ST-7913 -2015-INIT/en/pdf.

———. 2016. *Comprehensive Approach to External Conflicts and Crises—Action Plan 2016–17.* Brussels: Publications Office of the EU. http://data.consilium.europa.eu/doc/document/ST-11408-2016-INIT/en/pdf.

———. 2017a. *From Shared Vision to Common Action: Implementing the EU Global Strategy Year 1.* Brussels: Publications Office of the EU. http://europa.eu/globalstrategy/sites/globalstrategy/files/full_brochure _year_1.pdf.

———. 2017b. *Joint Communication to the European Parliament and the Council: A Strategic Approach to Resilience in the EU's External Action.* Brussels: Publications Office of the EU. https://eeas.europa.eu /sites/eeas/files/join_2017_21_f1_communication_from_commission_to_inst_en_v7_p1_916039.pdf.

European Parliament. 2007. *EU Response to Situations of Fragility in Developing Countries.* Brussels: Publications Office of the EU. http://www.europarl.europa.eu/sides/getDoc.do?pubRef=-//EP//TEXT+TA+P6 -TA-2007-0540+0+DOC+XML+V0//EN.

European Parliament and Council. 2017. *Regulation Establishing the European Fund for Sustainable Development (EFSD), the EFSD Guarantee and the EFSD Guarantee Fund.* Brussels: Publications Office of the EU. http://data.consilium.europa.eu/doc/document/PE-43-2017-INIT/en/pdf.

European Union. 2016. *Shared Vision, Common Action: A Stronger Europe—A Global Strategy for the European Union's Foreign and Security Policy.* Brussels: Publications Office of the EU. http://www.eeas .europa.eu/archives/docs/top_stories/pdf/eugs_review_web.pdf.

Faria, Fernanda. 2014. *What EU Comprehensive Approach? Challenges for the EU Action Plan and Beyond.* Maastricht: European Centre for Development Policy Management. http://ecdpm.org/wp-content /uploads/BN71-What-EU-Comprehensive-Approach-October-2014.pdf.

Federal Ministry for Economic Cooperation and Development. 2007. *Development-Oriented Transformation in Conditions of Fragile Statehood and Poor Government Performance.* Bonn: Federal Ministry for Economic Cooperation and Development. https://www.bmz.de/en/publications/archiv/type_of _publication/strategies/konzept153.pdf.

Ferreira, Ines A. 2015. "Defining and Measuring State Fragility: A New Proposal." Paper presented in Berkeley at the Annual Bank Conference on Africa. http://cega.berkeley.edu/assets/miscellaneous_files/109 _-_ABCA_2015_Ines_Ferreira_Defining_and_measuring_state_fragility__A_new_proposal_May15.pdf.

———. 2017. "Measuring State Fragility: A Review of the Theoretical Groundings of Existing Approaches." *Third World Quarterly* 38 (6): 1291–1309.

Friedman, Thomas. 2016. *Thank You for Being Late: An Optimist's Guide to Thriving in the Age of Accelerations.* New York: Farrar, Straus and Giroux.

Fund for Peace (FFP). 2014. *CAST Conflict Assessment Framework Manual.* Washington, DC: FFP. http://library.fundforpeace.org/library/cfsir1418-castmanual2014-english-03a.pdf.

——. 2015. *The World in 2015: Country-by-Country Trend Analysis.* Washington, DC: FFP. http://library.fundforpeace.org/blog-20150620-countrytrends.

——. 2017. *Fragile States Index 2017.* Washington, DC: FFP. https://reliefweb.int/sites/reliefweb.int/files/resources/951171705-Fragile-States-Index-Annual-Report-2017.pdf.

Furness, Mark. 2014. *Let's Get Comprehensive: European Union Engagement in Fragile and Conflict-Affected Countries.* Bonn: German Development Institute. https://www.die-gdi.de/uploads/media/DP_5.2014.pdf.

g7+. 2015. *Note on the Fragility Spectrum.* g7+. http://www.g7plus.org/sites/default/files/resources/g7%2B%2BEnglish%2BFS%2BNote%2BDesign.pdf.

Gelbard, Enrique. 2015. *Building Resilience in Sub-Saharan Africa's Fragile States.* Washington, DC: IMF. http://www.imf.org/en/Publications/Departmental-Papers-Policy-Papers/Issues/2016/12/31/Building-Resilience-in-Sub-Saharan-Africa-s-Fragile-States-42950.

Geneva Declaration on Armed Violence and Development. 2015. *Global Burden of Armed Violence 2015: Every Body Counts.* Geneva: Geneva Declaration on Armed Violence and Development. http://www.genevadeclaration.org/measurability/global-burden-of-armed-violence/global-burden-of-armed-violence-2015.html.

Ghani, Ashraf, and Clare Lockhart. 2008. *Fixing Fragile States: A Framework for Rebuilding a Fractured World.* New York: Oxford University Press.

Gilpin, Raymond. 2017. "Peace Economics in a Changing World." *Economics of Peace and Security Journal* 12 (2): 32–36.

Gisselquist, Rachel M. 2014. *Aid, Governance and Fragility.* Helsinki: UN University World Institute for Development Economics Research. https://www.wider.unu.edu/sites/default/files/PP2014-Aid%2C%20Governance%20and%20Fragility.pdf.

Goldstone, Jack A., Robert H. Bates, David L. Epstein, Ted Robert Gurr, Michael B. Lustik, Monty G. Marshall, Jay Ulfelder, and Mark Woodward. 2010. "A Global Model for Forecasting Political Instability." *American Journal of Political Science* 54 (1): 190–208. https://sites.duke.edu/niou/files/2011/06/goldstone-bates-etal.pdf.

Goldstone, Jack A., Ted Robert Gurr, Barbara Harff, Marc A. Levy, Monty G. Marshall, Robert H. Bates, David L. Epstein, Colin H. Kahl, Pamela T. Surko, John C. Ulfelder, Jr., and Alan N. Unger. 2000. *State Failure Task Force Report: Phase III Findings.* http://www.raulzelik.net/images/rztextarchiv/uniseminare/statefailure%20task%20force.pdf.

Governance and Social Development Resource Centre (GSDRC). 2010. *The World Bank in Fragile States.* Birmingham: GSDRC. http://www.gsdrc.org/docs/open/hd651.pdf.

Grimm, Sonja, Nicolas Lemay-Hebert, and Olivier Nay, Editors. 2015. *The Political Invention of Fragile States: The Power of Ideas.* New York: Routledge.

Hameed, Sadika, and Kathryn Mixon. 2013. *Private Sector Development in Fragile, Conflict-Affected, and Violent Countries.* Washington, DC: CSIS. https://csis-prod.s3.amazonaws.com/s3fs-public/legacy_files/files/publication/130617_Hameed_PrivateSecDevel_WEB.pdf.

Haq, Mahbub ul. 1995. *Reflections on Human Development*. New York: Oxford University Press.

Hauck, Volker, and Camilla Rocca. 2014. *Gaps between Comprehensive Approaches of the EU and EU Member States*. Maastricht: European Centre for Development Policy Management.

Haugen, Gary A., and Victor Boutros. 2014. *The Locust Effect: Why the End of Poverty Requires the End of Violence*. New York: Oxford University Press.

Hausmann, Ricardo, Dani Rodrik, and Andrés Velasco. 2006. "Getting the Diagnosis Right." *Finance and Development* 43 (1).

Hearn, Sarah. 2016. *Independent Review of the New Deal for Engagement in Fragile States*. New York: New York University Center on International Cooperation. http://cic.nyu.edu/sites/default/files/new _deal_engagement_hearn_apr14_final.pdf.

Hearn, Sarah, Alejandra Kubitschek Bujones, and Alischa Kugel. 2014. *The United Nations "Peacebuilding Architecture": Past, Present and Future*. New York: New York University Center on International Co-operation. http://cic.nyu.edu/sites/default/files/un_peace_architecture.pdf.

Her Majesty's Government. 2015. *National Security Strategy and Strategic Defence and Security Review 2015: A Secure and Prosperous United Kingdom*. London: Controller of Her Majesty's Stationery Office. https://www.gov.uk/government/uploads/system/uploads/attachment_data/file/478936/52309_Cm _9161_NSS_SD_Review_PRINT_only.pdf.

Her Majesty's Treasury and Department for International Development. 2015. *UK Aid: Tackling Global Challenges in the National Interest*. London: Chancellor of the Exchequer. https://www.gov.uk /government/uploads/system/uploads/attachment_data/file/478834/ODA_strategy_final_web_0905.pdf.

Hoffmann, Anette. 2014. *Policy Review: International and Dutch Policies in the Field of Socio-Economic Development in Fragile Settings*. Occasional Paper No. 10. Wageningen, the Netherlands: IS Academy on Human Security in Fragile States. https://www.clingendael.nl/sites/default/files/International%20 and%20Dutch%20policies%20in%20the%20field%20of%20socio-economic%20development%20in%20 fragile%20settings%20-%20Hoffmann.pdf.

Holmberg, Soren, and Bo Rothstein. 2012. *Good Government: The Relevance of Political Science*. Northampton, MA: Edward Elgar.

Hughes, Jacob, Ted Hooley, Siafa Hage, and George Ingram. 2014. *Implementing the New Deal for Fragile States*. Washington, DC: Brookings Institution. https://www.brookings.edu/wp-content/uploads/2014/07 /global_20160811_new_deal_fragile_states.pdf.

Human Security Report Project. 2014. *Human Security Report 2013: The Decline in Global Violence— Evidence, Explanation, and Contestation*. Vancouver, British Columbia: Human Security Press. https:// reliefweb.int/sites/reliefweb.int/files/resources/HSRP_Report_2013_140226_Web.pdf.

Ingram, George, and Jonathan Papoulidis. 2017. *Rethinking How to Reduce State Fragility*. Washington, DC: Brookings Institution. https://www.brookings.edu/blog/up-front/2017/03/29/rethinking-how-to-reduce -state-fragility.

Ingram, Sue. 2011. *State-Building: Key Concepts and Operational Implications in Two Fragile States—The Case of Sierra Leone and Liberia*. New York: UN Development Programme (UNDP) and World Bank. http://www.undp.org/content/undp/en/home/librarypage/crisis-prevention-and-recovery/statebuilding _conceptsandoperationalimplicationsintwofragilestat.html.

Institute for Economics and Peace. 2015. *Global Terrorism Index 2015: Measuring and Understanding the Impact of Terrorism*. Sydney: Institute for Economics and Peace. http://economicsandpeace.org/wp -content/uploads/2015/11/Global-Terrorism-Index-2015.pdf.

———. 2017a. *Global Peace Index 2017.* Sydney: Institute for Economics and Peace. http://visionofhumanity .org/app/uploads/2017/06/GPI-2017-Report-1.pdf.

———. 2017b. *Global Terrorism Index 2017: Measuring and Understanding the Impact of Terrorism*. Sydney: Institute for Economics and Peace. http://visionofhumanity.org/app/uploads/2017/11/Global-Terrorism -Index-2017.pdf.

Institute for State Effectiveness. 2009. *Institutional Reform of Development Organizations—Case Study: African Development Bank*. Washington, DC: Institute for State Effectiveness. http://stateeffective .wpengine.com/wp-content/uploads/2015/09/Institutional-Reform-of-Development-Organizations.pdf.

International Development Association (IDA). 2016. *Special Theme: Fragility, Conflict and Violence*. Wash- ington, DC: World Bank, http://documents.worldbank.org/curated/en/652991468196733026/pdf/106182 -BR-IDA18-Fragility-Conflict-and-Violence-PUBLIC-IDA-R2016-0140.pdf.

———. 2017. *Towards 2030: Investing in Growth, Resilience and Opportunity*. Report from the Executive Directors of the International Development Association to the Board of Governors. Washington, DC: World Bank, http://documents.worldbank.org/curated/en/348661486654455091/pdf/112728-correct -file-PUBLIC-Rpt-from-EDs-Additions-to-IDA-Resources-2-9-17-For-Disclosure.pdf.

International Dialogue on Peacekeeping and Statebuilding (IDPS). 2011. *A New Deal for Engagement in Fragile States*. Paris: IDPS. http://www.pbsbdialogue.org/media/filer_public/07/69/07692de0-3557-494e -918e-18df00e9ef73/the_new_deal.pdf.

———. 2014a. *Guidance Note on Fragility Assessments*. Paris: IDPS. http://www.pbsbdialogue.org/media/filer _public/96/fb/96fb5ae4-7b0d-4007-bf9e-1ed869db21da/rd_4_fragility_assessment_guidance_note _final.pdf.

———. 2014b. *New Deal Monitoring Report 2014*. Paris: IDPS. http://www.pbsbdialogue.org/media/filer _public/a5/df/a5dfd621-00a5-4836-8e20-8fff3afd1187/final_2014_new_deal_monitoring_report.pdf.

———. 2016. *Stockholm Declaration on Addressing Fragility and Building Peace in a Changed World*. Paris: IDPS. http://www.government.se/contentassets/8c2491b60d494dd8a2c1046b9336ee52/stockholm -declaration-on-addressing-fragility-and-building-peace-in-a-changing-world.pdf.

International Institute for Strategic Studies. 2017. *Armed Conflict Survey 2017.* London: International Institute for Strategic Studies.

International Monetary Fund (IMF). 2008. *The Fund's Engagement in Fragile States and Post-Conflict Countries: A Review of Experience—Issues and Options*. Washington, DC: IMF. https://www.imf.org /external/np/pp/eng/2008/030308.pdf.

———. 2011. *Macroeconomic and Operational Challenges in Countries in Fragile Situations*. Washington, DC: IMF. https://www.imf.org/external/np/pp/eng/2011/061511a.pdf.

———. 2012. *Staff Guidance Note on the Fund's Engagement with Countries in Fragile Situations*. Washing- ton, DC: IMF. http://www.imf.org/external/np/pp/eng/2012/042512.pdf.

———. 2015. *IMF Engagement with Countries in Post-Conflict and Fragile Situations—A Stocktaking*. Wash- ington, DC: IMF. https://www.imf.org/external/np/pp/eng/2015/050715.pdf.

——. 2016a. *Financing for Development: Enhancing the Financial Safety Net for Developing Countries—Further Considerations*. Washington, DC: IMF. https://www.imf.org/en/Publications/Policy-Papers/Issues/2016/12/31/Financing-for-Development-Enhancing-the-Financial-Safety-Net-for-Developing-Countries-PP5076.

——. 2016b. *Fact Sheet: Financing the IMF's Concessional Lending to Low-Income Countries*. Washington, DC: IMF. http://www.imf.org/external/np/exr/facts/pdf/concesslending.pdf.

——. 2017a. *Building Fiscal Capacity in Fragile States*. Washington, DC: IMF. http://www.imf.org/en/Publications/Policy-Papers/Issues/2017/06/14/pp041817building-fiscal-capacity-in-fragile-state?cid=em-COM-123-35417.

——. 2017b. *The IMF and Fragile States: Issues Paper for an Evaluation by the Independent Evaluation Office*. Washington, DC: IMFd. http://www.ieo-imf.org/ieo/files/whatsnew/FS_Final%20Issues_Paper%207-25-17.pdf.

Joint Chiefs of Staff. 2013. *Counterinsurgency*. Joint Publication 3-24. Washington, DC: Department of Defense. http://www.dtic.mil/doctrine/new_pubs/jp3_24.pdf.

——. 2014. *Counterterrorism*. Joint Publication 3-26. Washington, DC: Department of Defense. http://www.dtic.mil/doctrine/new_pubs/jp3_26.pdf.

——. 2016. *Stability*. Joint Publication 3-07. Washington, DC: Department of Defense. http://www.dtic.mil/doctrine/new_pubs/jp3_07.pdf.

Kaplan, Seth D. 2008. *Fixing Fragile States*. Westport, CT: Praeger Security International.

——. 2013. *Betrayed: Politics, Power, and Prosperity*. New York: Palgrave Macmillan.

——. 2017. "Weak States: When Should We Worry?" *The American Interest* 12 (4). http://www.the-american-interest.com/2017/01/26/weak-states-when-should-we-worry.

Killick, Tony, with Ramani Gunatilaka and Ana Marr. 1998. *Aid and the Political Economy of Policy Change*. New York: Routledge.

Kleinfeld, Rachel. 2017. *Reducing All Violent Deaths, Everywhere: Why the Data Must Improve*. Washington, DC: Carnegie Endowment for International Peace. http://carnegieendowment.org/files/CP_297_Kleinfeld_Crime_Final_Web.pdf.

LaFree, Gary, Laura Dugan, and Erin Miller. 2015. *Putting Terrorism in Context: Lessons from the Global Terrorism Database*. New York: Routledge.

Liang, Junwei, Susanne Burger, Alex Hauptmann, and Jay D. Aronson. 2016. *Video Synchronization and Sound Search for Human Rights Documentation and Conflict Monitoring*. Pittsburg: Carnegie Mellon University. https://www.cmu.edu/chrs/documents/Video-Synchronization-Technical-Report.pdf.

Liu, Chaoying, and Emily Harwit. 2016. *The Effectiveness of Private Sector Development Interventions in Fragile and Conflict-Affected Situations: Evidence from Evaluations*. Washington, DC: International Finance Corporation, World Bank. https://openknowledge.worldbank.org/bitstream/handle/10986/28497/120073-WP-Systematic-review-of-PSD-interventions-in-FCS-PUBLIC.pdf?sequence=1&isAllowed=y.

Maddison, Angus. 2001. *The World Economy: A Millennial Perspective*. Paris: Organization for Economic Cooperation and Development (OECD).

Mandaville, Alicia Phillips. 2016. *Applying the Compact Model of Economic Assistance in Fragile States*. Washington, DC: US Institute of Peace. https://www.usip.org/sites/default/files/Fragility -Report-Policy-Brief-Applying-Compact-Model-of-Economic-Assistance-in-Fragile-States_0 .pdf.

Marc, Alexandre. 2016. *Conflict and Violence in the 21st Century: Current Trends as Observed in Empirical Research and Statistics*. Washington, DC: World Bank. http://www.un.org/pga/70/wp-content/uploads /sites/10/2016/01/Conflict-and-violence-in-the-21st-century-Current-trends-as-observed-in-empirical -research-and-statistics-Mr.-Alexandre-Marc-Chief-Specialist-Fragility-Conflict-and-Violence-World -Bank-Group.pdf.

Marc, Alexandre, Alys Wilklman, Ghazia Aslam, Michelle Rebosio, and Kanishka Balasuriya. 2013. *Societal Dynamics of Fragility: Engaging Societies in Responding to Fragile Situations*. Washington, DC: World Bank. https://openknowledge.worldbank.org/handle/10986/12222.

Margolis, J. Eli. 2012. "Following Trends and Triggers: Estimating State Instability." *Studies in Intelligence* 56 (1): 13–24. https://www.cia.gov/library/center-for-the-study-of-intelligence/csi-publications/csi-studies /studies/vol.-56-no.-1/pdfs-vol-56.-no.-1/Estimating%20State%20Instability%20-Extracts-Mar12-20Apr12 .pdf.

Marshall, Monty G., and Benjamin R. Cole. 2014. *Global Report 2014: Conflict, Governance, and State Fragility*. Vienna, VA: Center for Systemic Peace.

Marshall, Monty G., and Gabrielle Elzinga Marshall. 2016. *State Fragility Index and Matrix 2015*. Vienna, VA: Center for Systemic Peace. http://www.systemicpeace.org/inscr/SFImatrix2015c.pdf.

McGee, Rosemary, and Celestine Kroesschell. 2013. *Local Accountabilities in Fragile Contexts: Experiences from Nepal, Bangladesh and Mozambique*. Brighton: Institute of Development Studies. http://www.ids .ac.uk/files/dmfile/Wp422.pdf.

Mcloughlin, Claire. 2012. *Topic Guide on Fragile States*. Birmingham: GSDRC. http://www.gsdrc.org/docs /open/con86.pdf.

Melander, Erik. 2015. *Organized Violence in the World 2015*. Uppsala: Conflict Data Program. http://www .pcr.uu.se/digitalAssets/61/c_61335-l_1-k_brochure2.pdf.

Michel, James. 2016. *Beyond Aid: The Integration of Sustainable Development in a Coherent International Agenda*. Washington, DC: CSIS. https://csis-prod.s3.amazonaws.com/s3fs-public/legacy_files/files /publication/160111_Michel_BeyondAid_Web.pdf.

Ministry of Foreign Affairs, Ministry of Defence, Ministry of Justice. 2013. *Denmark's Integrated Stabilization Engagement in Fragile and Conflict-Affected Areas of the World*. Copenhagen: Danish International Development Agency. http://danida-publikationer.dk/upload/microsites/um/ebooks/stabiliseringspolitik _uk_web.pdf.

Moser, Caroline, and Ailsa Winton. 2002. *Violence in the Central American Region: Towards an Integrated Framework for Violence Reduction*. London: Overseas Development Institute. https://www.odi.org/sites /odi.org.uk/files/odi-assets/publications-opinion-files/1826.pdf.

Muggah, Robert, Timothy D. Sisk, Eugenia Piza-Lopez, Jago Salmon, and Patrick Keuleers 2012. *Governance for Peace: Securing the Social Contract*. New York: UN Development Program. http://www.undp .org/content/undp/en/home/librarypage/crisis-prevention-and-recovery/governance_for_peace securingthesocialcontract.html.

Multilateral Development Bank Working Group. 2007. *Toward a More Harmonized Approach to MDB Engagement in Fragile Situations*. Washington, DC: World Bank. http://siteresources.worldbank.org /INTLICUS/Resources/Report_of_the_MDB_Working_Group.pdf.

National Audit Office. 2017. *Managing the Official Development Assistance Target—A Report on Progress*. London: National Audit Office. https://www.nao.org.uk/wp-content/uploads/2017/07/Managing-the -Official-development-Assistance-target-a-report-on-progress-Summary.pdf.

National Intelligence Council. 2017. *Global Trends: Paradox of Progress*. Washington, DC: National Intelligence Council. http://www.dni.gov/nic/globaltrends.

Norris, John. 2016. *A Better Approach to Fragile States: The Long View*. Washington, DC: Center for American Progress. https://cdn.americanprogress.org/wp-content/uploads/2016/06/20123009/LongView FragileStates-report.pdf.

Norris, John, Casey Dunning, and Annie Malknecht. 2015. *Fragile Progress: The Record of the Millennium Development Goals in States Affected by Conflict, Fragility, and Crisis*. Washington, DC: Center for American Progress and Save the Children. http://www.savethechildren.org/atf/cf/%7B9def2ebe-10ae -432c-9bd0-df91d2eba74a%7D/FRAGILESTATES-REPORT_WEB.PDF.

North, Douglass C., John Joseph Wallis, Steven B. Webb, and Barry R. Weingast. 2007. *Limited Access Orders in the Developing World: A New Approach to the Problems of Development*. Washington, DC: World Bank. https://openknowledge.worldbank.org/bitstream/handle/10986/7341/WPS4359.pdf ?sequence=1&isAllowed=y.

——. 2013. *In the Shadow of Violence: Politics, Economics, and the Problems of Development*. New York: Cambridge University Press.

North, Douglass C., John Joseph Wallis, and Barry R. Weingast. 2013. *Violence and Social Orders: A Conceptual Framework for Interpreting Recorded Human History*. New York: Cambridge University Press (paperback edition).

Nyheim, David. 2009. *Preventing Violence, War and State Collapse: The Future of Conflict Early Warning and Response*. Paris: OECD. https://www.oecd.org/dac/conflict-fragility-resilience/docs/preventing%20 violence%20war%20and%20state%20collapse.pdf.

Odendaal, Andries. 2012. *The Road to the New Deal: Working Papers, 2010–2011 International Dialogue Working Groups*. International Dialogue for Peacebuilding and Statebuilding. https://www.pbsbdialogue .org/media/filer_public/3f/ef/3fef42cb-88cb-43d3-ad3b-c248b1bb261a/the_road_to_the_new_deal.pdf.

Organization for Economic Cooperation and Development (OECD). 1996. *Shaping the 21st Century: The Contribution of Development Co-operation*. Paris: OECD. https://www.oecd.org/dac/2508761.pdf.

——. 1998. *Development Cooperation Report 1997: Efforts and Policies of the Members of the Development Assistance Committee*. Paris: OECD. http://www.oecd-ilibrary.org/docserver/download /4398011e.pdf?expires=1505403379&id=id&accname=guest&checksum=3F86E49EEF47B78F7B9CC0 79D85D8C0C.

——. 2001. "Conflict, Peace and Development Cooperation on the Threshold of the 21st Century," published in *Preventing Violent Conflict (2001)*. Paris: OECD.

——. 2003. "Working for Development in Difficult Partnerships," in *2002 Development Cooperation Report*, 153–164. Paris: OECD. http://www.oecd-ilibrary.org/docserver/download/4303311e.pdf?expires=150618 4960&id=id&accname=guest&checksum=C6CE3BE92B4EB62255710019A100B370.

——. 2007. *Principles for Good International Engagement in Fragile States & Situations.* Paris: OECD. http://www.oecd.org/dac/conflict-fragility-resilience/docs/38368714.pdf.

——. 2010a. *Do No Harm: International Support for Statebuilding.* Paris: OECD. https://www.oecd.org/dac/conflict-fragility-resilience/docs/do%20no%20harm.pdf.

——. 2010b. *Monitoring the Principles for Good International Engagement in Fragile States and Situations: Global Report.* Paris: OECD. http://www.keepeek.com/Digital-Asset-Management/oecd/development/monitoring-the-principles-for-good-international-engagement-in-fragile-states-and-situations_9789264090057-en#.WSii04WcHIU#page1.

——. 2015. *States of Fragility 2015.* Paris: OECD. http://www.oecd-ilibrary.org/docserver/download/4315011e.pdf?expires=1503686954&id=id&accname=guest&checksum=7B3DE0D4B9E08DB39B3DDA864E576C02.

——. 2016a. *Good Development Support in Fragile, At-Risk and Crisis-Affected Contexts.* Paris: OECD. http://www.oecd-ilibrary.org/docserver/download/5jm0v3s71fs5-en.pdf?expires=1495834258&id=id&accname=guest&checksum=532D556653116777C3CD938624F0801B.

——. 2016b. *States of Fragility 2016.* Paris: OECD. http://www.oecd-ilibrary.org/docserver/download/4316101e.pdf?expires=1503687162&id=id&accname=guest&checksum=F238BADDB1ED3A081A57A0BC3DFEADD3.

Organization for Economic Cooperation and Development and World Economic Forum. 2015. *Blended Finance Vol. 1: A Primer for Development Finance and Philanthropic Funders.* Geneva: World Economic Forum. http://www3.weforum.org/docs/WEF_Blended_Finance_A_Primer_Development_Finance_Philanthropic_Funders.pdf.

Overseas Private Investment Corporation (OPIC). 2014. *Seven Approaches to Developing Projects in Fragile Governance Environments.* Washington, DC: OPIC. https://www.opic.gov/sites/default/files/files/Fragile%20Governance%20Advisory%20Note.pdf.

Owuor, Victor Odundo. 2017. *Firm Behavior in Fragile States.* Broomfield, CO: One Earth Future Foundation. http://oefresearch.org/sites/default/files/documents/publications/Firm_Behavior_Fragile_States.pdf.

Paris Declaration on Aid Effectiveness. 2005. Paris: OECD. http://www.oecd.org/dac/effectiveness/34428351.pdf.

Patrick, Stewart. 2008. "U.S. Policy toward Fragile States: An Integrated Approach to Security and Development." In *The White House and the World: A Global Development Agenda for the Next U.S. President,* edited by Nancy Birdsall. Washington, DC: Center for Global Development, 327–353.

——. 2011. *Weak Links: Fragile States, Global Threats, and International Security.* New York: Oxford University Press.

Perkins, Dwight A., Steven Radelet, David L. Lindauer, and Steven A. Block. 2013. *Economics of Development.* New York: W.W. Norton & Company.

Peschka, Mary Porter. 2011. *The Role of the Private Sector in Fragile and Conflict-Affected States.* Washington, DC: World Bank. http://documents.worldbank.org/curated/en/887641468163482532/pdf/620590WP0The0R0BOX0361475B00PUBLIC0.pdf.

Pham, Phuong N., and Patrick Vinck. 2012. "Technology, Conflict, Early Warning Systems, Public Health, and Human Rights." *Health and Human Rights* 14 (2): 106–117, at 115. https://cdn2.sph.harvard.edu/wp-content/uploads/sites/13/2013/06/Pham-FINAL2.pdf.

Piffaretti, Nadia, Laura Ralston, and Khadija Shaikh. 2014. *Information Note: The World Bank Group's Harmonized List of Fragile Situations*. Washington, DC: World Bank. http://documents.worldbank.org/curated/en/692741468338471327/Information-note-the-World-Banks-harmonized-list-of-fragile-situations.

Pinker, Steven. 2011. *The Better Angels of Our Nature: Why Violence Has Declined*. New York: Viking, Penguin Group.

Pinker, Steven, and Andrew Mack. 2014. "The World Is Not Falling Apart: Never Mind the Headlines. We've Never Lived in Such Peaceful Times." *Slate*. http://www.slate.com/articles/news_and_politics/foreigners/2014/12/the_world_is_not_falling_apart_the_trend_lines_reveal_an_increasingly_peaceful.html.

Pritchett, Lant, and Frauke de Weijer. 2010. *Fragile States: Stuck in a Capability Trap?* Washington, DC: World Bank. http://siteresources.worldbank.org/EXTWDR2011/Resources/6406082-1283882418764/WDR_Background_Paper_Pritchett.pdf.

Radelet, Steven. 2015. *The Great Surge: The Ascent of the Developing World*. New York: Simon and Schuster.

Rao, Sumedh. 2014. *Problem-Driven Iterative Approaches and Wider Governance Reform*. Birmingham: GSDRC. http://gsdrc.org/docs/open/hdq1099.pdf.

Rausch, Colette, ed. 2017. *Fighting Serious Crimes: Strategies and Tactics for Conflict-Affected Societies*. Washington, DC: U.S. Institute of Peace.

Reece, Maite. 2017. "Measuring Fragile States: Are the Rankings Really Different?" The Hague: Netherlands Institute of International Relations. https://www.clingendael.org/pub/2017/monitor2017/crises_fragile_states/pdf/crises_fragile_states_appendix.pdf. (Appendix to *Crises: Fragile States; Thematic Study, Clingendael Strategic Monitor 2017*, by Kars de Bruijne. The Hague: Netherlands Institute of International Relations. https://www.clingendael.nl/sites/default/files/clingendael_strategic_monitor_2017_crises_fragile_states.pdf.)

Rice, Susan, and Stewart Patrick. 2008. *Index of State Weakness in the Developing World*. Washington, DC: Brookings Institution.

Rocha de Siqueira, Isabel. 2017. *Managing State Fragility: Conflict, Quantification and Power*. New York: Routledge.

Rohwerder, Brigitte. 2015. *Conflict Early Warning and Early Response*. Birmingham: GDSRC. *Helpdesk Research Report*. Institute of Development Studies. http://www.gsdrc.org/docs/open/hdq1195.pdf.

Rosand, Eric. 2016. *Communities First: A Blueprint for Organizing and Sustaining a Global Movement against Violent Extremism*. Washington, DC: The Prevention Project: Organizing against Violent Extremism. http://www.organizingagainstve.org/wp-content/uploads/2016/12/Communities_First_December_2016.pdf.

Runde, Daniel. 2017. *A Tale of Two Paths: Divergence in Development*. Washington, DC: CSIS. https://csis-prod.s3.amazonaws.com/s3fs-public/publication/170227_Runde_DivergentDevelopmentLandscape_Web_0.pdf?XwSBfmApDe9ISHvuXb8aGhuSHVcsrIbx.

Sen, Amartya. 1999. *Development as Freedom*. New York: Knopf.

Slotin, Jenna, and Molly Elgin-Cossart. 2013. *Why Would Peace Be Controversial at the United Nations? Negotiations toward a Post-2015 Development Framework*. New York: New York University Center on

International Cooperation. http://cic.nyu.edu/sites/default/files/negotiations_post_2015_dev _framework.pdf.

Smith, Stephen C. 2015. "The Two Fragilities: Vulnerability to Conflict, Environmental Stress, and Their Interaction as Challenges to Ending Poverty." In *The Last Mile in Ending Extreme Poverty*, edited by Chandy, Laurence, Hiroshi Kato, and Homi Kharas. Washington, DC: Brookings Institution.

Stamnes, Eli, and Kari M. Osland. 2016. *Synthesis Report: Reviewing UN Peace Operations, the UN Peacebuilding Architecture and the Implementation of UNSCR 1325*. Oslo: Norwegian Institute of International Affairs. http://www.un.org/pga/70/wp-content/uploads/sites/10/2016/01/NUPI_Report_2_16 _Stamnes_Osland.pdf.

Stepputat, Finn, and Lauren Greenwood. 2013. *Whole-of-Government Approaches to Fragile States and Situations*. Copenhagen: Danish Institute for International Studies. http://pure.diis.dk/ws/files/46447/DIIS _RP2013_25_Stepputat_Web.pdf.

Stewart, Frances, and Graham Brown. 2009. *Fragile States*. Oxford: Center for Research on Inequality, Human Security and Ethnicity. https://assets.publishing.service.gov.uk/media/57a08b62e5274a27b2000 af7/wp51.pdf.

Tella, Oluwaseun. 2016. "AFRICOM: Hard or Soft Power Initiative?" *African Security Review* 25 (4): 393–406.

Tikuisis, Peter, and David Carment. 2017. *Categorization of States beyond Strong and Weak*. Ottawa: Carleton University. https://carleton.ca/cifp/wp-content/uploads/1549.pdf.

Tschirgi, Necia, and Cedric de Coning. 2015. *Ensuring Sustainable Peace: Strengthening Global Security and Justice through the UN Peacebuilding Architecture*. Washington, DC, and The Hague: Commission on Global Security, Justice and Governance. https://www.stimson.org/sites/default/files/Commission_BP _Tschirgi_De-Coning.pdf.

United Nations (UN). 1992a. *An Agenda for Peace: Preventive Diplomacy, Peacemaking, and Peacekeeping*. Report of the Secretary General. UN Doc. A/47/277–S/24111. New York: UN. http://www.un.org/ga /search/view_doc.asp?symbol=A/47/277.

———. 1992b. *An Agenda for Peace: Preventive Diplomacy, Peacebuilding and Peace-Making*. UNGA Res. 47/120. New York: UN. http://www.un.org/documents/ga/res/47/a47r120.htm.

———. 1994. *An Agenda for Development*. UNGA Res. 48/166. New York: UN. http://www.un-documents.net /a48r166.htm.

———. 1996. *An Agenda for Democratization*. UNGA Doc. A/51/761. New York: UN. http://www.un.org/fr /events/democracyday/pdf/An_agenda_for_democratization.pdf.

———. 2000a. *Report of the Panel on United Nations Peace Operations*. UN Doc. A/55/305, S/2000/809. New York: UN. http://www.un.org/en/ga/search/view_doc.asp?symbol=A/55/305.

———. 2000b. *Women, Peace and Security*. UNSC Res. 1325. New York: UN. https://documents-dds-ny.un .org/doc/UNDOC/GEN/N00/720/18/PDF/N0072018.pdf?OpenElement.

———. 2000c. *United Nations Millennium Declaration*. UNGA Res. 55/2. New York: UN. https://undocs.org /A/RES/55/2.

———. 2004. *A More Secure World: Our Shared Responsibility*. Report of the Secretary-General's High-level Panel on Threats, Challenges and Change. New York: UN. http://www.un.org/en/peacebuilding/pdf /historical/hlp_more_secure_world.pdf.

——. 2005a. *In Larger Freedom: Towards Development, Security and Human Rights for All*. UN Doc. A/59/2005. New York: UN. https://documents-dds-ny.un.org/doc/UNDOC/GEN/N05/270/78/PDF /N0527078.pdf?OpenElement.

——. 2005b. *2005 World Summit Outcome*. UNGA Res. 60/1. New York: UN. http://www.un.org/women watch/ods/A-RES-60-1-E.pdf.

——. 2005c. *The Peacebuilding Commission*. UNGA Res. 60/180. New York: UN. http://www.un.org/ga /search/view_doc.asp?symbol=A/RES/60/180.

——. 2009. *Report of the Secretary General on Peacebuilding in the Immediate Aftermath of Conflict*. UN Doc. A/63/881–S/2009/304. New York: UN. http://www.un.org/en/peacebuilding/pbso/pdf/s2009304.pdf.

——. 2010. *Review of the United Nations Peacebuilding Architecture*. UN Doc. A/64/868–S/2010/393. New York: UN. http://www.un.org/ga/search/view_doc.asp?symbol=A/64/868.

——. 2015a. *Report of the High-Level Independent Panel on Peace Operations on Uniting Our Strengths for Peace: Politics, Partnership and People*. UN Doc. A/70/95—S/2015/446. New York: UN. http://www .un.org/en/ga/search/view_doc.asp?symbol=S/2015/446.

——. 2015b. *Challenge of Sustaining Peace: Report of the Advisory Group of Experts on the Review of the Peacebuilding Architecture*. UN Doc. A/69/968—S/2015/490. New York: UN. http://www.un.org/ga /search/view_doc.asp?symbol=A/69/968.

——. 2015c. *The Future of United Nations Peace Operations: Implementation of the Recommendations of the High-Level Independent Panel on Peace Operations; Report of the Secretary-General*. UN Doc. A/70/357—S/2015/682. New York: UN. http://www.un.org/en/ga/search/view_doc.asp?symbol=S/2015 /682.

——. 2015d. *Plan of Action to Prevent Violent Extremism: Report of the Secretary-General*. UN Doc. A/70/674. New York: UN. http://www.un.org/en/ga/search/view_doc.asp?symbol=A/70/674.

——. 2015e. *Women, Peace, and Security*. UNSC Res. 2242. New York: UN. http://www.securitycouncilreport .org/atf/cf/%7B65BFCF9B-6D27-4E9C-8CD3-CF6E4FF96FF9%7D/s_res_2242.pdf.

——. 2015f. *Transforming Our World: The 2030 Agenda for Sustainable Development*. UNGA Res. 70/1. New York: UN. https://documents-dds-ny.un.org/doc/UNDOC/GEN/N15/291/89/PDF/N1529189.pdf ?OpenElement.

——. 2016a. *Report of the Secretary-General on Women and Peace and Security*. UN Doc. S/2016/822. New York: UN. http://www.un.org/en/ga/search/view_doc.asp?symbol=S/2016/822.

——. 2016b. *The Sustainable Development Goals Report 2016*. New York: UN. http://unstats.un.org/sdgs /report/2016/The%20Sustainable%20Development%20Goals%20Report%202016.pdf.

——. 2016c. *Review of the United Nations Peacebuilding Architecture*. UNGA Res.70/262. New York: UN. http://www.un.org/en/ga/search/view_doc.asp?symbol=A/RES/70/262.

——. 2017a. *Summary of Key Messages and Observations from the High-Level Dialogue on "Building Sustainable Peace for All: Synergies between the 2030 Agenda for Sustainable Development and Sustaining Peace."* New York: UN. http://www.un.org/pga/71/wp-content/uploads/sites/40/2015/08 /Summary-of-the-High-level-Dialogue-on-Building-Sustainable-Peace-for-All.pdf.

——. 2017b. *The Sustainable Development Goals Report 2017*. New York: UN. https://unstats.un.org/sdgs /files/report/2017/TheSustainableDevelopmentGoalsReport2017.pdf.

United Nations Development Programme (UNDP). 2005. *Human Development Report 2005*. New York: UNDP. http://hdr.undp.org/sites/default/files/reports/266/hdr05_complete.pdf.

———. 2012. *Governance for Peace: Securing the Social Contract*. New York: UNDP. http://www.undp.org/content/undp/en/home/librarypage/crisis-prevention-and-recovery/governance_for_peacesecuringthesocialcontract.html.

———. 2016a. *New Deal Implementation Support Facility: 2015 Annual Report*. New York: UNDP. http://www.undp.org/content/undp/en/home/librarypage/democratic-governance/undp-new-deal-facility-annual-report-2015.html.

———. 2016b. *UNDP Support to the Implementation of Sustainable Development Goal 16*. New York: UNDP. http://www.undp.org/content/dam/norway/undp-ogc/documents/16_peace_Jan15_digital.pdf.

———. 2016c. *Arab Human Development Report 2016: Youth and the Prospects for Human Development in a Changing Reality*. New York: UNDP.

———. 2016d. *Building Inclusive Societies and Sustaining Peace through Democratic Governance and Conflict Prevention: An Integrated Approach*. New York: UN. http://www.undp.org/content/undp/en/home/librarypage/democratic-governance/building-inclusive-societies-and-sustaining-peace-through-democr.html.

———. 2017. *Journey to Extremism in Africa: Drivers, Incentives and the Tipping Point for Recruitment*. New York: UNDP. http://journey-to-extremism.undp.org/content/downloads/UNDP-JourneyToExtremisim-report-2017-english.pdf.

United Nations High Commissioner for Refugees (UNHCR). 2017. *Global Trends: Forced Displacement in 2016*. Geneva: UNHCR. http://www.unhcr.org/5943e8a34.

United States Agency for International Development (USAID). 2005a. *Fragile States Strategy*. Washington, DC: USAID. http://pdf.usaid.gov/pdf_docs/PDACA999.pdf.

———. 2005b. *Measuring Fragility: Indicators and Methods for Rating State Performance*. Washington, DC: USAID. http://pdf.usaid.gov/pdf_docs/Pnadd462.pdf.

———. 2005c. *Fragile States Indicators: A Supplement to the Country Analytical Template*. Washington, DC: USAID. http://pdf.usaid.gov/pdf_docs/Pnadg262.pdf.

———. 2011. *The Development Response to Violent Extremism and Insurgency*. Washington, DC: USAID. https://www.usaid.gov/sites/default/files/documents/1870/VEI_Policy_Final.pdf.

———. 2012a. *Building Resilience to Recurrent Crisis*. Washington, DC: USAID. https://www.usaid.gov/sites/default/files/documents/1870/USAIDResiliencePolicyGuidanceDocument.pdf.

———. 2012b. *Local Systems: A Framework for Supporting Sustained Development*. Washington, DC: USAID. https://www.usaid.gov/policy/local-systems-framework.

———. 2014. *Ending Extreme Poverty in Fragile Contexts*. Washington, DC: USAID. http://pdf.usaid.gov/pdf_docs/pnaec864.pdf.

———. 2015. *USAID Policy on Cooperation with the Department of Defense*. Washington, DC: USAID. https://www.usaid.gov/sites/default/files/documents/1866/USAIDPolicyCooperationDoD.pdf.

———. 2016. Automated Directives System Chapter 201. "Program Cycle Operational Policy." Washington, DC: USAID. https://www.usaid.gov/ads/policy/200/201.

United States National Security Strategy. 2015. Washington, DC: National Archives. https://obamawhitehouse.archives.gov/sites/default/files/docs/2015_national_security_strategy_2.pdf

U.S. Institute of Peace. 2016. "Policy Briefs: U.S. Leadership and the Challenge of State Fragility." http://www.usip.org/fragilitypolicybriefs.

U.S. Institute of Peace and U.S. Army Peacekeeping and Stability Operations Institute. 2009. *Guiding Principles for Stabilization and Reconstruction*. Washington, DC: United States Institute for Peace. https://www.usip.org/sites/default/files/guiding_principles_full.pdf.

Van Zanden, Jan Luiten, Joerg Baten, Marco Mira d'Ercole, Auke Rijpma, Conal Smith, and Marcel Timmer. 2014. *How Was Life? Global Well-Being since 1820*. Paris: OECD.

Vilalta, Carlos. 2015. *Global Trends and Projections of Homicidal Violence, 2000 to 2030*. Rio de Janeiro: Igarapé Institute. https://igarape.org.br/wp-content/uploads/2016/04/Homicide-Dispatch_2_EN_22-04-16.pdf.

Weingast, Barry R. 2009. *Why Are Developing Countries so Resistant to the Rule of Law?* Florence: European University Institute. http://cadmus.eui.eu/bitstream/handle/1814/11173/MWP_LS_2009_02.pdf?sequence=1&isAllowed=y.

Weiss, Stefani, Hans-Joachim Spanger, and Wim van Meurs, editors. 2009. *Diplomacy, Development and Defense: A Paradigm for Policy Coherence—A Comparative Analysis of International Strategies*. Gütersloh: Verlag Bertelsmann Stiftung.

Wittkowsky, Andreas, and Ulrich Wittkampf. 2013. *Pioneering the Comprehensive Approach: How Germany's Partners Do It*. Berlin: Center for International Peace Operations. http://www.zif-berlin.org/fileadmin/uploads/analyse/dokumente/veroeffentlichungen/ZIF_Policy_Briefing_Andreas_Wittkowsky_Ulrich_Wittkampf_Jan_2013.pdf.

World Bank. 1998. *Post-Conflict Reconstruction: The Role of the World Bank*. Washington, DC: World Bank. http://documents.worldbank.org/curated/pt/175771468198561613/pdf/multi-page.pdf.

———. 2002. *World Bank Group Work in Low-Income Countries under Stress: A Task Force Report*. Washington, DC: World Bank. http://documents.worldbank.org/curated/en/329261468782159006/World-Bank-Group-work-in-low-income-countries-under-stress-a-task-force-report.

———. 2004. *Practical Guide to Multilateral Needs Assessments in Post-Conflict Situations*. Washington, DC: World Bank. http://documents.worldbank.org/curated/en/224281468762594718/pdf/298220PAPER0SDP0WP151Web.pdf.

———. 2007. *Operational Approaches and Financing in Fragile States*. Washington, DC: World Bank. http://siteresources.worldbank.org/IDA/Resources/IDA15FragileStates.pdf.

———. 2011a. *World Development Report 2011: Conflict, Security, and Development*. Washington, DC: World Bank. https://siteresources.worldbank.org/INTWDRS/Resources/WDR2011_Full_Text.pdf.

———. 2011b. *Operationalizing the 2011 World Development Report: Conflict, Security, and Development*. Washington, DC: World Bank. http://siteresources.worldbank.org/DEVCOMMINT/Documentation/22884392/DC2011-0003(E)WDR2011.pdf.

———. 2014a. *Fragility and Conflict: Changing the Paradigm*. Washington, DC: World Bank. http://siteresources.worldbank.org/EXTLICUS/Resources/sixpoints-brochure.pdf.

——. 2014b. *World Bank Group Assistance to Low-Income Fragile and Conflicted-Affected States: An Independent Evaluation.* Washington, DC: World Bank. https://ieg.worldbankgroup.org/Data/Evaluation/files/fcs_eval.pdf.

——. 2014c. *Promoting Foreign Investment in Fragile and Conflict-Affected Situations.* Washington, DC: World Bank. https://openknowledge.worldbank.org/bitstream/handle/10986/20432/911900BRI0Box30 D0VC0KNOWLEDGE0NOTES.pdf?sequence=1&isAllowed=y.

——. 2016. *World Bank Group Engagement in Situations of Fragility, Conflict, and Violence: An Independent Evaluation.* Washington, DC: World Bank. https://openknowledge.worldbank.org/bitstream/handle/10986/24915/World0Bank0Gro0dependent0evaluation.pdf?sequence=4&isAllowed=y.

——. 2017. *World Development Report 2017: Governance and the Law.* Washington, DC: World Bank. https://openknowledge.worldbank.org/handle/10986/25880.

World Bank and International Monetary Fund Development Committee. 2017b. *Forward Look—A Vision of the World Bank Group in 2030: Progress and Challenges.* Washington, DC: World Bank. http://siteresources.worldbank.org/DEVCOMMINT/Documentation/23745169/DC2017-0002.pdf.

World Bank and UN. 2017. *Pathways for Peace: Inclusive Approaches to Preventing Violent Conflict—Main Messages and Emerging Policy Directions.* Washington, DC: World Bank. https://openknowledge.worldbank.org/bitstream/handle/10986/28337/211162mm.pdf?sequence=2&isAllowed=y.

World Economic Forum. 2014. *The Role of the Private Sector in Fragile States: Catalyzing Investment for Security and Development.* Geneva: World Economic Forum. http://www3.weforum.org/docs/GAC14/WEF_GAC14_FragileStatesConflictPrevention_Report%20.pdf.

——. 2016a. *Responsible Private Sector Action to Address Fragility, Conflict and Violence.* Geneva: World Economic Forum. http://www3.weforum.org/docs/WEF_Responsible_Private_Sector.pdf.

——. 2016b. *The Global Risks Report 2016.* Geneva: World Economic Forum. http://www3.weforum.org/docs/Media/TheGlobalRisksReport2016.pdf.

World Health Organization, United Nations Office on Drugs and Crime, United Nations Development Program. 2014. *Global Status Report on Violence Prevention 2014.* Geneva: World Health Organization. http://www.who.int/violence_injury_prevention/violence/status_report/2014/report/report/en.

About the Author

James Michel is a senior adviser with the CSIS Project on Prosperity and Development and an independent consultant in development cooperation. Ambassador Michel's long career in public service has included service as deputy legal adviser, U.S. Department of State (1977–1982); principal deputy assistant secretary of state for Inter-American affairs (1983–1987); U.S. ambassador to Guatemala (1987–1989); and in USAID, as assistant administrator for Latin America and the Caribbean (1990–1992); acting deputy administrator and acting administrator (1992–1993); and counselor to the agency (1999–2000 and 2009–2010). From 1994 to 1999 he was chair of the OECD Development Assistance Committee. In the private sector he was senior counsel to Tetra Tech DPK, an international consulting firm, from 2003 to 2009. He received his JD cum laude from Sai Louis University. He is the author of *Beyond Aid: The Integration of Sustainable Development in Coherent International Agenda* (CSIS, January 2016).